Brewing Everything

THE COUNTRYMAN PRESS
A division of W. W. Norton & Company
Independent Publishers Since 1923

Brewing Everything

DAN CRISSMAN

How to Make Your Own Beer, Cider, Mead, Sake, Kombucha, and Other Fermented Beverages

Disclaimer: This volume is intended as a general information resource. Brewing beverages at home carries certain risks, including, but not limited to, contamination of beverages from inadequate sanitization of equipment, allergic reactions to ingredients, and burns and back strain from moving heavy containers of hot liquids. See the author's note for a more detailed list of the risks and how to minimize them. As of press time, the URLs displayed in this book link or refer to existing websites. The publisher is not responsible for, and should not be deemed to endorse or recommend, any website other than its own or any content not created by it, nor is the author responsible for any third-party material.

For information about permission to reproduce selections from this book, write to Permissions, The Countryman Press, 500 Fifth Avenue, New York, NY 10110

For information about special discounts for bulk purchases, please contact W. W. Norton Special Sales at specialsales@wwnorton.com or 800-233-4830

Manufacturing by Versa Press
Series book design by Nick Caruso Design
Production manager: Devon Zahn

The Countryman Press
www.countrymanpress.com

A division of W. W. Norton & Company, Inc.
500 Fifth Avenue, New York, NY 10110
www.wwnorton.com

978-1-68268-174-9 (pbk.)

10 9 8 7 6 5 4 3 2 1

Photo Credits

page 7: ©ClaudeMic/iStockPhoto.com; 8: ©rasilja/iStockPhoto.com; 20: ©adamkaz/iStockPhoto.com; 23: ©Wavebreakmedia/iStockPhoto.com; 25: ©LlCreate/iStockPhoto.com; 26: ©zmurciuk_k/iStockPhoto.com; 29: ©LlCreate/iStockPhoto.com; 34: ©rasilja/iStockPhoto.com; 49: ©IrisImages/iStockPhoto.com; 50: ©rasilja/iStockPhoto.com; 74: ©LlCreate/iStockPhoto.com; 76: ©heysooooos/iStockPhoto.com; 79: ©Veronika Roosimaa/iStockPhoto.com; 82: ©Arianna Carli/iStockPhoto.com; 88: ©javitrapero/iStockPhoto.com; 90: ©fauxgt4/iStockPhoto.com; 93: ©Achudo/iStockPhoto.com; 97: ©tverkhovinets/iStockPhoto.com; 102: ©Boogich/iStockPhoto.com; 104: ©Osuleo/iStockPhoto.com; 107: ©yanik88/iStockPhoto.com; 111: ©Westhoff/iStockPhoto.com; 120: ©bdspn/iStockPhoto.com; 130: ©takasuu/iStockPhoto.com; 137: ©whitemay/iStockPhoto.com; 154: ©taka4332/iStockPhoto.com; 156: ©GreenArt Photography/iStockPhoto.com; 159: ©shanecotee/iStockPhoto.com; 165: ©princessdlaf/iStockPhoto.com; 170: ©balhash/iStockPhoto.com; 173: ©JessieEldora/iStockPhoto.com; 175: ©luknaja/iStockPhoto.com; 180: ©PhoebeMillerDesign/iStockPhoto.com; 188: ©MmeEmil/iStockphoto.com

Brewing at home is incredibly fun and satisfying. But you need to always be aware of certain safety risks and to take precautions to minimize them.

- **ALWAYS BE SANITIZING!**
  - Fermentation, which is the process by which beer and other drinks are brewed, literally involves growing and harnessing microbes, otherwise known as germs. This means that the brewing process does involve some risk of attracting unwanted mold or bacteria. But if you properly sanitize your equipment at the start and at each step along the way, you can minimize the risk of contamination. (Proper sanitizing also can protect against off flavors in the finished product.) Yeast, which is the key ingredient in most of these beverages, is a very strong organism, and in most conditions, as long as you are continually sanitizing, the yeast will naturally outcompete any bad bacteria.
  - One popular sanitizing solution that I like is an acid-based, no-rinse brand called Star San, but there are other effective products such as iodine solutions. I recommend avoiding bleach or chlorine solutions, as they can impart unpleasant aromas or flavors to the finished brew. Whichever solution you use, just follow the directions on the bottle. Most sanitizing solutions come in concentrated form: you add a small amount of the sanitizer to a bucket of water and submerge the equipment you want to sanitize for at least a few minutes. Boiling your equipment for several minutes is another way to kill anything you might not want.
- **MOLD:** If, despite your best sanitizing efforts, you do see mold in or on one of your creations, throw the brew out immediately.
- **ALLERGIES TO INGREDIENTS:** If you're brewing for yourself, obviously you shouldn't include any ingredient to which you know you're allergic. Beer that includes lactose should not be served to anyone who is lactose intolerant or sensitive to dairy. If you want to serve a home-brewed beverage to someone who is allergic to gluten, try cider or mead, which are naturally gluten free, unless you add malt to them.
- **FRESHNESS OF INGREDIENTS:** Make sure bottled juice or any other packaged ingredient is not past its sale date. Examine apples and other fresh ingredients to make sure they are not stale.
- **EXPLODING BOTTLES:** You may have heard people talk about exploding home-brew bottles. Bottles do sometimes explode, but this happens relatively rarely, and when it does happen, it's generally caused by pressure building up over time, after you've set your brew aside to ferment. The risk of a bottle explosion is really quite low as long as you follow the sugar measurements

given in the recipes, but I recommend storing brew bottles in a closed space to lessen the possibility of damage or injury from flying glass if an explosion does occur.

- **INJURIES FROM CARRYING HEAVY CONTAINERS:** Large batches of beverages can be quite heavy. Use common sense to avoid back strain when you are lifting and moving pots of brew, as, for example, when transferring a pot into an ice bath.

- **BURNS/SCALDING:** You also will be handling boiling or very hot liquid a lot, like when you transfer the contents of the pot to a sanitized bucket or glass jug or drain liquid from mash into another container. Use common sense to avoid burns: keep your face well away from steam, and wear protective clothing (e.g., oven mitts and insulated aprons) as appropriate to prevent injury.

CONTENTS

Brewing Made Simple— and Then Harder

Like so many others, I got into fermentation through beer. The notion of turning four simple ingredients—water, malt, hops, and yeast—into a delicious, intoxicating beverage seemed like magic to me, and I wanted to know more about the process. So I toured some breweries, read some guidebooks, and finally worked up the nerve to brew my own. And my first try wasn't bad! (It wasn't good, either.)

Quickly, I realized that the same natural engine that gives us beer powers all kinds of other processes as well. Add a bit of yeast to apple juice, and you have hard cider. Do the same to honey and water, and you have mead. Bacteria, which we've all been raised from birth to fear, are responsible for some of the healthiest and most delicious drinks in the world.

So what is this magical thing we call fermentation? Put simply, fermentation is one of many natural processes that break down one thing into another. Fermentation is what turns cabbage into sauerkraut,

milk into cheese, and a casing of ground pork into spicy soppressata. Fermentation gives bread its lift and vinegar its bite. It is a process that is happening all around us all the time. It may sound like a gross overstatement, but it is no exaggeration to say that learning how to nurture this natural phenomenon is one of the cornerstones of human civilization. Before the first refrigerator ever rolled off the assembly line, fermentation was how we kept food stable and healthy all year round.

But beyond gifting us with the holy combination

of cheese and bread, fermentation is also responsible for another cornerstone of civilization: alcohol. The basic outlines are simple: Sugar + Water + Microbes = Alcohol + Carbon Dioxide. The term "microbes" encompasses yeast, bacteria, and other small organisms that do the heavy lifting of fermentation. Floating in a sweet liquid, these microbes feast on the stored energy in carbohydrate molecules, turning the sugars into booze and bubbles. The key to brewing is understanding what your chosen microbe likes to eat, at what temperature it feels most cozy, and which other organisms it plays well with. The endless variations on that equation are bounded only by your own creativity and understanding of nature.

When I realized how simple it was to do this at home, I became obsessed. Soon my kitchen became half-laboratory, with gurgling glass jugs hiding behind every cabinet door. I made my own kimchi and yogurt and lox (much to the chagrin of my better half). But fermented beverages were my real passion. It dawned on me after some trial and error that, in today's world, there are two ways to brew pretty much any fermented drink: the easy way and the hard way. Often these roughly correspond to "the new way" and "the old-fashioned way," but there are elements of modern convenience in both. If you know how the process works, you can start wherever you want.

Brewing Everything walks you through the process from start to finish, beginning with easier shortcuts until you get the hang of it and then upgrading to the harder stuff. Following this introduction, you'll find information on useful gear that every brewer should have in their kitchen. The first four chapters each take on one core beverage—beer, cider, mead, and sake—that every homebrewer can and should make. The Easy Way sections get you accustomed to the broad outlines of the process and include 1-gallon batch recipes to try first, until you get the hang of it. Then, the Hard Way sections up the ante, teaching you how the pros—or, at least, the learned amateurs—do it. Because these methods are more advanced and typically require additional (and sometimes expensive) equipment, the recipes that follow the Hard Way scale up the batch size. After all, if you're going to do it the hard way, why not make enough to last?

The last chapter features a selection of healthy, mostly nonalcoholic ferments that follow similar processes to their alcoholic cousins, but are a little simpler to make. The most famous of these is likely kombucha, prized by hippies everywhere for the digestive benefits of its healing probiotics. The dirty little secret about probiotics, though, is that you'll actually find them, in some form, in every single recipe in this book. All homebrew is naturally probiotic, since that simply refers to the living microorganisms that power fermentation. Besides being responsible for tasty ales and dry ciders, yeast is also a potent nutrient that is great for your gut.

Every chapter in *Brewing Everything* also features tips and insights gleaned from experts such as brewmasters, cider-makers, new meadery start-

ups, and small-batch kombucha sellers. Nearly all the professionals who make the brews you love so much started out as homebrewers, just like you. As Malcolm Gladwell's famous 10,000 Hour Rule attests, enough practice will make you truly great at anything you set your mind to. And trust me, once you get the hang of fermentation, you won't need 10,000 hours to become an expert brewer. It's way too easy for that!

Speaking of experts, I should state right off the bat that this book is largely aimed at novices rather than experienced brewers. If your basement is already replete with old water-cooler mash tuns and box after box of empty bottles waiting to be filled—that is to say, if your basement looks like mine—there is an ever-growing library of more technical homebrewing books that may be better suited to your specific questions about, say, chemical water treatments or malic acid conversion. Most experienced brewers, though, tend to specialize in one particular beverage, or even one particular style of that beverage. If that describes you, this book can help you step out of your comfort zone. The descriptions of each method are written to highlight which parts of the process are similar to your preferred craft, and which ones are different. So if you've been perfecting your hazy New England IPA recipe for years but have never tried to make sake, give it a try. I assure you, you can do it.

In short, *Brewing Everything* is about making your favorite drinks from scratch, but letting you decide at what point "scratch" begins. Whether you use a sugary malt syrup or a bag of barley, the result is a cool, foamy glass of ale. You can pick and press apples from the orchard, or you can let the farmhands do the hard part for you and still sip a fantastic cider. Not a fan of bees? Store-bought honey will make a killer mead. The key is understanding how it all works, how to make it safe, and how to create the ideal environment for the yeast or bacteria to work their magic. Then you can sit back and reap the rewards.

BREWING GEAR

As with any hobby, home fermentation can lead to the accumulation of unnecessary gadgets designed to make things easier. Before we get started, let's take a moment to go over some of the actual essentials of any brewer's kitchen, as opposed to the useless Christmas gifts your mom will get for you once she learns you make beer.

Essentials

Fermentation vessel: Some sort of vessel to ferment is the only truly essential piece of equipment for all of these beverages. Use a vessel that is at least 10 percent bigger than the yield of your batch, to allow for headspace. Many of the commercially available homebrew vessels account for this, so a "5-gallon" container will likely hold about 5½ gallons of liquid. But it's always best to measure first to make sure you know just how much your container holds.

The shape and material of this vessel is totally up to you, but big, food-grade plastic buckets and glass carboys are the most common. Buckets are much easier to clean without a special bottle brush, but yeast and bacteria from previous batches can get stuck in scratches or grooves on the sides. Glass carboys are harder to wash but much more resistant to these hangers-on, and their transparent nature allows you to observe the fermentation process in all its glory. Either way, as long as you keep your equip-

ment cleaned and sanitized after each batch, you shouldn't have any issues.

Stockpot: A large stockpot is a must-have for home-brewing, especially when making beer. It should preferably be stainless steel and hold about twice as much volume as the final batch size. So if you're brewing 3 gallons, you'll want a pot that holds 6 gallons. This kind of pot is also useful for mead, but less so for cider or sake.

Sanitizing solution: A clean and sterile environment is a required starting point for all fermentations. There are many different kinds of food-grade sanitizers you can use, so pick the one that works best for you. (See *Safety* on page 19.)

Spoon: Preferably a big one with a long handle that can reach to the bottom of your pot or fermentation vessel for stirring. Metal or heat-resistant plastic (instead of wood) are best in order to avoid contamination.

Bung: The key to making an airtight seal on your fermenter is a rubber stopper or grommet that fits the hole in your fermentation vessel of choice.

Airlock: This is just a little plastic piece that allows gas to exit, but not enter. There are a few different styles, but as long as you can add water to it, you should be fine.

Siphoning via hose into a perfectly fitting strainer and funnel

Siphon: A siphon, or racking cane, is the easiest and best way to transfer liquids from one container to another without spillage. Siphoning also limits your fermented beverage's exposure to oxygen, which can affect its shelf life. If you're fermenting in a carboy, this is pretty much essential when it comes to bottling. But either way, a siphon makes transferring cleaner, safer, and more efficient. And do yourself a favor—buy an auto-siphon. (See my rant on page 21).

Strainer: A metal, wire-mesh strainer helps filter out all the stuff you don't want in the final brew.

Funnel: Narrow-necked containers are a big part of the brewing process, and filling them effectively requires a large funnel. Make sure your wire-mesh strainer can fit neatly and securely in the top of the funnel, as you'll often be using them together.

Hose: If you're using a siphon, you need a hose. The cheapest ones are vinyl, but the heat-resistant silicone hoses are ideal for transferring hot liquids.

Hose clamp: This little piece fits on the end of the

hose and allows you to stop the flow of liquid when siphoning or bottling.

Bottles: Once your beverages are fully fermented, you'll need to bottle them. You can use any cleaned (and sanitized!) old glass bottle, provided it doesn't have a twist-off style threaded lip.

Bottling wand: A rigid plastic tube that fits into the end of your hose, this makes bottling infinitely easier and cuts down on potential spillage.

Capper and caps: You can buy bottle caps and a capper from any homebrew supply shop. If you buy swing-top style, self-capping bottles (think Grolsch), you can skip this.

Cheesecloth or Muslin: This permeable cloth is amazingly useful in all types of fermentation. From holding steeping grains to separating rice lees from sake, this is a truly indispensable staple.

Kitchen scale: The precise measurements of some common ingredients used in fermentation can be extremely annoying to convert into teaspoons or tablespoons. It can also be confusing when dealing with ounces in both weight (dry ounces) and volume (fluid ounces). Take the guesswork out of all of it with a digital kitchen scale. They're super cheap, and the batteries last forever.

Optional, but Nice to Have

Instant-read thermometer: These digital probes offer an exact reading of the temperature of your liquid. Since they're often made of metal, sanitizing is a snap. This is almost a must-have for fermentation, and if you enjoy cooking at all, you should have one of these anyway.

Hydrometer: To know the final alcohol content of your beverage, you need to measure the sugar you start with and how much is left after fermentation. A hydrometer—a small glass tube that floats—easily measures the specific gravity of any solution with a simple twist. Take a reading at the start and at the end; the difference will give you the alcohol by volume.

Wine thief: Rather than trying to pour samples from a full bucket or carboy, a wine thief allows you to grab a little bit of liquid for tasting or testing without any legwork. It is a long glass or plastic tube with a small opening at one end and a tapered point at the other that works like a giant straw. Just dip it and put your finger over top to close the seal.

pH test strips: For some fermentations, especially cider, it can be useful to know how acidic your solution is. Home pH test strips made from litmus paper are easy to find and easy to use. When a drop of liquid is added, the color of the strip will change according to its pH, which you can determine by comparing the strip to the color chart provided with it.

Yeast nutrient: Conventional wisdom says that for yeast to perform at its best you'll need to add this powdered nutrient mix, which is predominantly made of ammonium phosphate and food-grade urea (yum!), to fermentations such as ciders and meads. But in practice, I've found that as long as you're using enough healthy yeast, you'll be fine without it.

Bottle brush: Cleaning up post-fermentation can be a real pain, especially inside glass jars with narrow tops. A bottle brush helps get into those hard-to-reach places.

Heating pad: Sometimes you need to warm up the environment for your precious little microbes, and an electric heating pad is a simple, low-cost way to do so.

Totally Unnecessary, but Super Cool

Refractometer: If you want to be a fancypants and tell your friends about the Brix in your fruit (don't ask, you really don't need to know when you're first starting out), then this expensive gadget is the way to go. Like a hydrometer, it measures the sugar content (specific gravity) of any liquid. But unlike a hydrometer, it requires only a tiny drop of said liquid rather than a few ounces.

Immersion chiller or counterflow plate: These typically copper contraptions aid with quick cooling of liquids. Most useful in making beer, they hook up to a cold-water source and allow for heat exchange without any new liquid entering the solution. They can be a huge time-saver for beer brewers, but a big investment. And really, an ice bath works just as well, even though it takes a little longer.

Sous vide machine: These cylindrical water bath heaters are all the rage in this post–Iron Chef world. A sous vide machine serves the same purpose as a much less expensive heating pad, but it also offers much more control. You can dial in the exact temperature. You can also make truly amazing rare steaks with it, so why not?

Stir plate: If you want your fermentation setup to resemble an actual science lab, this heating plate fit for an Erlenmeyer flask is perfect. With its magnetic stirring rod (that looks disturbingly like a horse tranquilizer pill) it is undeniably useful for ensuring proper aeration and temperature in a yeast starter. But it's also a bulky, ugly appliance that serves no other purpose in the kitchen unless you want to be Walter White and break bad.

BREWING TECHNIQUES

While there are many procedures specific to each individual brew, there are a few common threads that run through all of them. Here, we'll delve into some important techniques that will come in handy no matter what you're brewing.

Safety: ABS (Always Be Sanitizing!)

People are often scared by the idea of fermentation, since it boils down to growing and harnessing microbes. But if you properly sanitize your equipment at the start and at each step along the way, there's almost no risk involved. Yeast is a very strong organism, and in most conditions it will naturally outcompete any bad bacteria. I can't stress this enough, though: Always sanitize your equipment! See the Author's Note on page 5 for more safety recommendations and sanitizing tips.

Making a Yeast Starter

No matter what beverage you're making, starting with healthy and active yeast ensures that fermentation will begin quickly and continue without any hiccups. Aside from doubling the amount of commercial yeast you add to the brew—which can get expensive—the best way to do this is by making a yeast starter.

To make a starter, sanitize a quart-sized Mason jar and add boiling water along with an appropriate sugar in a roughly 10-to-1 ratio. You want the yeast to get used to the type of sugar that it will later eat on a larger scale, so a yeast starter is essentially a mini version of whatever batch you want to make. If you're making beer, make a starter with malt extract. This simple syrup starter also works when you're making cider, or you can just use an equal amount of pasteurized juice in place of the sugar and water mixture. If you're making mead, use a starter with honey. If you're making sake, ideally you would use some sort of rice mixture, but as you'll see when we get there that can be a very labor-intensive process. Better to just use simple table sugar along with a couple of teaspoons of yeast nutrient, which will grow the yeast without adding any other flavors.

Once the sugar and hot water are mixed together into a solution, set the jar aside and let it cool to room temperature. Then stir in the yeast. Place a piece of cheesecloth or muslin over the mouth of the jar and secure it with a rubber band or the outer ring of the canning lid. Let it sit overnight on the day before your intended brew day, and by morning you should see bubbles climbing up the side of the jar. That little fizzing noise tells you the yeast is ready to tackle whatever batch you have planned for it.

Temperature Control

Most of the recipes in this book are tailored toward yeasts that do their best work at standard room temperature, around 70°F, but the more you branch out the more you'll find that yeast can be quite finicky. Controlling the temperature of your medium is the single best way to improve the overall quality of your fermentation.

It is also the most annoying way. Unless you live somewhere with a root cellar that stays cool in the summer but still warm enough in winter, you will struggle to find a spot in your home with a consistent temperature of around 50°F, which is ideal for lager beers, sake, and some ciders. You will also find it challenging to keep temperatures in the upper 80s and 90s, which is great for farmhouse beers and koji rice cultures.

Ingenious homebrewers who've come before us have tackled this problem in myriad ways. You can buy electronic temperature regulators that hook up to old fridges and freezers, kicking them on and off to maintain a constant cool temperature of your choice inside. You can also buy warming belts to wrap around your fermentation vessel to keep the yeast nice and toasty.

My advice, though? Don't go all in on these right off the bat. Adjust your brewing to your environment, not the other way around. Find styles you like that work well in your space. Do you live in the frozen tundra? Maybe lagers are right for you. Own a desert ranch? Try saison. (Or turn up that powerful

central air-conditioning unit you undoubtedly have.) It will save money, but it will also be truer to your brew's sense of place.

Racking

Because fermented beverages are best when minimally exposed to oxygen, the preferred method for moving any of your final products from their fermentation vessels is through siphoning, also called racking. Thus, before you start messing with yeast, it's best to learn how to do this effectively.

The premise is simple: Use a tube to pull the liquid from one container to the next. To do this, you need some force on the lower end of the tube to get the flow started. If you've ever siphoned gas out of a gas tank (or seen a movie where someone does it), you know that one way to do this is by sucking on the end of the tube like a straw. This often ends

An auto-siphon ready for racking

with a mouthful of said liquid, though. A mouthful of beer might not sound so bad, but putting your microbe-filled mouth on the end of the tube will likely lead to contamination. (Remember: Always Be Sanitizing!)

So how do you generate that force without suction? Water. The quick flow of liquid out of one end of the tube naturally pulls the rest of the liquid along with it, thanks to gravity and hydrostatic pressure. First, place the sanitized racking cane into your fermentation vessel with the hooked end sticking out the top. Then, add water to the hose, holding it in a U-shape so that the liquid fills the hose completely. Carefully attach one end of the hose to the racking cane, spilling as little water as possible. Then position the container you want to transfer the brew into below the vessel, and quickly drop the other end of the tube into it. The force of the rushing water

will grab the brew in the vessel and pull it along for the ride.

The above instruction is fairly intuitive once you get the hang of it, but let me impart one piece of sage advice before we continue: Buy an auto-siphon. Seriously. Auto-siphons are just like regular racking canes, except that they sit in an open-ended casing tube. This tube allows you to create a closed system, so that raising the cane pulls air into the container and lowering it pushes air—and your liquid—out. A few quick up-and-down pumps on the cane thus creates the same siphoning force that the full tube of water does in the more traditional method.

You may be like the old me and think, "No, I'm smart. I'm capable. I can do this the normal way." But then you'll be four-fifths of the way through racking a 5-gallon carboy full of hoppy IPA and you'll accidentally nudge the racking cane just a hair. "Ah, it'll be fine," you'll think. Then suddenly, the flow will stop. You'll then spend the next half-hour trying to get the liquid flowing smoothly again, but it won't because it is MUCH harder to rack when the liquid level in the carboy is low. You'll then give up and try to just pour the rest of it out, inadvertently pouring the yeasty sludge and hop residue that had settled at the bottom of the carboy into your previously pristine brew. You'll curse the sky and wonder why you were foolish enough not to just buy an auto-siphon, which would allow you to easily get it all flowing again with a few quick pumps of the cane.

Don't be like the old me. Buy an auto-siphon.

Bottling

Once you've mastered siphoning, you can move on to bottling. The premise is the same—moving liquid between containers—but in this case you're moving from one larger container to many smaller ones.

While you can bottle directly from your fermentation vessel, it's often easier to move into a secondary container first. You can buy buckets with a built-in spigot at the bottom for easy bottling, or you can just buy the spigot and make one at home by drilling a hole in any bucket. Some form of bottling bucket is highly recommended, as it avoids the potential headaches that come from stopping and starting racking. (See the previous rant.)

If you plan to carbonate your brew in the bottle, add some more sugar to the solution or to each bottle to reignite the fermentation process. This is referred to as priming sugar. A general rule of thumb is 1 ounce of sugar per gallon of liquid, but you can adjust this up or down depending on the level of carbonation you want. To ensure even distribution of the priming sugar in each bottle, it is best to dilute it in a few ounces of water before adding it to your brew. Heating the sugar and water in a saucepan to make a simple syrup is even better, since that will also pasteurize the mixture—though make sure to cool it down before adding it to your brew. Then you can either rack your brew onto the sugar, or evenly divide the sugar solution among all your bottles. More sugar means more bubbles, but be careful not to overdo it lest you end up with the homebrewer's greatest fear—the exploding bottle. If you stick close to the 1 gallon-to-1 ounce ratio, this really shouldn't be a concern. Since the buildup of pressure in the bottle happens over time, store the bottles in a closed space such as a closet or cabinet just to be on the safe side.

Whether you are carbonating or not, moving your brew from big container to small bottle requires either a hose clamp or a bottling wand to avoid spillage. Clean, sanitize, and set up all your bottles within reach of your hose and start the flow. Fill each bottle almost to the top, but make sure to leave an inch or so of headspace. Then, cap each bottle, either using the swing-top self-sealers or crown-style with a capper.

If you want a still beverage (sans bubbles), then fill the bottles without any added sugar and pasteurize by soaking them in a 170°F water bath for at least 15 minutes. If carbonating, add the proper amount of sugar and let them sit for at least 2 weeks in a cool, dark place before opening. This is what brewers refer to as *bottle conditioning*.

While the amount of sugar you add will be the determining factor in the level of carbonation, how you store the bottles—and how long you let them sit—is important, too. Essentially, bottle conditioning is an extension of the fermentation process on a smaller scale. The yeast that turned your sugary concoction into an alcoholic elixir is still alive and floating around in the liquid. When it eats the new sugar you've given it, carbon dioxide will be given off once again, only now because of the cap it has no place to escape. Over time, the gas builds up in the headspace at the top of the bottle, and is then reabsorbed into the liquid as carbonation. It is for this reason that you want to store the bottles for roughly the same amount of time and in roughly the same conditions under which you fermented the whole batch the first time around.

Kegging

For the advanced homebrewer, kegging allows you to store and serve large batches of brew without the hassle of bottling. You can buy old soda kegs, called

Cornelius kegs (or Corny kegs, for short), online or in most homebrew shops. These kegs were mass produced by Coke and Pepsi, each with their own particular set of fittings for intake and dispensing—typically referred to as either "ball lock" (Pepsi) or "pin lock" (Coke). Make sure you know what kind of keg you have before you purchase the fittings. For some reason, ball lock kegs are vastly more common among brewers, so going with that will make it much easier to find the right fittings at your local store.

Once you have the kegs and the fittings, you need something to hook them up to. Empty CO_2 tanks can be purchased online and exchanged for full tanks at any welding or gas supply store. Attach a regulator valve that allows you to set the pressure, (roughly 10 to 15 psi is a good rule of thumb), a gas tubing line (thick, red vinyl tubes available at any homebrew shop or hardware store), and the ball lock or pin lock fitting for the side of your keg labeled "in," and you can forgo the whole conditioning process and simply force-carbonate the whole batch to your desired level of effervescence. This can be a little intimidating the first time you hook this up, so I recommend watching some YouTube instructional videos on how to properly connect a gas tank to you keg to ensure no leakage. On the dispensing side, you can buy a simple picnic tap that dispenses with a mere squeeze of the hand. Store the keg and the gas tank in a small refrigerator, and you'll have a steady supply of cool and

Corny keg vs. commercial keg

delicious homebrew with none of the fuss of bottling. If you want to go all out, you can also buy (or make) your own kegerator with a tower and tap for the true home bar experience. A word of caution for all you hardcore DIYers, though: Making your own kegerator requires drilling into a commercial refrigerator, which can be incredibly dangerous if you don't know what you're doing. I've watched several fantastic YouTube explainers on the process, and I'm still far too scared to try this myself. I ordered a pre-built kegerator online and have never regretted it.

CHAPTER 1

Beer

Although beer is one of the more complicated brews, it makes sense to start this book with it. Beer is most people's first foray into the world of homebrewing. It is the gateway drug of fermentation.

When you think about it, this is completely unsurprising. Beer has been a staple of the human diet for as long as wine, and these days it inspires the same cultish following. But unlike wine, making good beer does not require specialized training or expert horticultural skills. All you need is access to four simple ingredients—grain, water, hops, and yeast.

From those four ingredients, you can make endless different styles. Pilsner. Hefeweizen. Stout. Porter. Dubbel. Tripel. Barleywine. Saison. Bière de Garde. Bière de Miel. Bock. Doppelbock. Roggenbier. Märzen. Kölsch. Berliner Weisse. Gose. Gueuze. Lambic. IPA. Pale Ale. Red Ale. Amber Ale. Brown Ale. Scotch Ale. Old Ale. Abbey Ale. The list goes on and on.

But no matter which beer you choose to make, the process is pretty much the same. Steep the grains to release their sugars. Boil and add hops to flavor. Ferment to make it alcoholic. Do those things in the right combination, and you can make anything you want.

An increasing number of homebrewers have done just that. In fact, the craft beer explosion over the past few decades owes a debt to the homebrewing community, particularly to American brewers. Forced to stomach mass-produced light lagers or pay through the nose for quality imports, intrepid Americans of all stripes fired up their brew kettles and forged a new culture.

But the outrageous success of craft beer is now taking its toll on homebrewing. With the incredible selection out there, what's the point in slaving over a hot stove on your weekend off? Isn't it easier just to stroll over to the local craft beer bar (pretty much every town has one now) and see what's on tap?

It begs the question—is homebrewing still relevant? I put this to Derek Dellinger, a longtime homebrewer who opened a farm brewery in 2015 in Kent, Connecticut. "While it can feel like we've run through every style of beer under the sun recently, homebrewers will always be on the forefront of experimentation due to the lack of restraints," says Dellinger. "As a professional brewer, you weigh so many factors in deciding what to brew next: cost of ingredients, availability of ingredients, how well you think a beer will sell, how seasonal that beer may be. A brewery has to brew for the market, to at least some extent, while a homebrewer can brew purely for themselves. And a 5-gallon batch of beer gone bad is not nearly so big of a deal as a 1,000-gallon production batch that doesn't turn out."

The economic argument for homebrewing is still compelling. True, there is more good beer being made professionally than ever before. But for the really cool and interesting stuff, you still have to pay a premium. Would you rather pay $10 for a tiny snifter of bourbon-aged imperial stout, or would you prefer to make gallons of it yourself for a fraction of the price? Or, as Dellinger put it, "If you want something popular and hard to find, like a great New England IPA, wouldn't you rather be able to craft five gallons of it at home instead of driving for hours and waiting in line to pick up a case?"

The freedom homebrewers enjoy can actually drive market trends, too. "Homebrewers were big on gose before that style of salty, sour wheat beer hit the market in a big way," Dellinger told me. "More and more, brewers need to focus on a few popular styles to stay relevant. So if you like a style of beer that's becoming obscure once again, your best bet is always brewing at home."

More importantly, though, homebrewing is fun! Like other kinds of cooking, you're creating something that tastes great and putting your own stamp on it. Brewing is an endlessly creative hobby that encourages experimentation. That's how Dellinger got into it: "Brewing combined so many things I already enjoyed: a sense of exploration, of discovering new things, digging up ancient secrets, crafting recipes, tinkering with gadgets, and connecting with a massive community of affable, like-minded peers. And soon, I realized the appeal of being able to brew beers that weren't readily available in stores. I was making my own kombucha and cider as well, and saw how much crossover potential there was, both in terms of similar flavor profiles or even blending two things together to create something entirely unique.

"With something so versatile and complex," Dellinger asked, "why wouldn't you want to personalize it to the greatest degree possible?"

The Easy Way

With this simple method, you can make delicious beer without ever touching the main ingredient:

much to use for the right taste in the finished beer is a delicate art.

STEEPING GRAINS

While you can make beer using only malt extract, steeping grains help you to adjust the flavors more precisely. If you want to brew a brown ale, for example, you can use "golden" extract and then add some roasted malts ("caramel" or "crystal" varieties) for depth and color. Just measure out what you need, crush the grains gently, pack them into a muslin bag, and add them straight to your liquid.

HOPS

These magical green cones are what give beer the bitterness and aroma we all crave. The flavor comes from the essential oils, and boiling helps to extract them. While you can buy dried whole-leaf hops, the vast majority of commercially available hops come

grain. *Extract brewing* allows you to skip the first step of the traditional brewing process, mashing the grain to draw out residual sugars. Here's what you'll need to get started.

MALT EXTRACT

Malt extract comes in two forms—dry powder or liquid syrup—and many different styles and variations. All of the major malting companies sell their own brand of extract in an assortment of flavors. If you want to make a pilsner or pale ale you can buy a "light, " "pale," or "golden" variety, or for a stout or porter you can pick up "amber" or "dark" ones. The problem with extract is that the flavors are all very one-note. The difference between "dark" and "extra dark" can be tough to discern, so knowing how

Common Hop Varieties

NAME	TYPICAL BEER STYLES	GOOD FOR	SMELL	SUBSTITUTIONS
Amarillo	Pale ale, IPA	Aroma	Citrus, fresh-cut flowers	Cascade, Centennial
Apollo	Pale ale, IPA	Bittering	Orange peel, bong resin	Summit
Azacca	Pale ale, IPA	Aroma	Tangerine, mango, pineapple	Citra
Brewer's Gold	Brown ale, German-style lager	Aroma	Black currant, spice	Northern Brewer, Galena
Cascade	All styles, most commonly pale ale and IPA	Bittering, Aroma	Pleasant, flowery, spicy, citrusy	Centennial, Amarillo, Columbus
Centennial	All styles, most commonly pale ale and IPA	Bittering, Aroma	Like Cascade, but stronger	Cascade, Columbus
Chinook	Pale ale, IPA, stout, porter	Bittering, Aroma	Pine, grapefruit	Nugget, Columbus, Northern Brewer
Citra	Pale ale, IPA	Aroma	Tropical fruit and citrus	Galaxy, Centennial, Nelson Sauvin
Cluster	Lager	Bittering	Quite spicy	Galena
Columbus	IPA, pale ale, stout	Bittering, Aroma	Pungent, dank, citrusy	Centennial
Fuggle	Porter, ESB, pale ale	Aroma	Mild and pleasant, earthy, fruity	Willamette, Styrian Golding
Galaxy	Pale ale, IPA	Aroma	Passionfruit, peach, mango	Citra, Amarillo, Centennial
Galena	Ale, porter, stout, ESB, bitter	Bittering	Clean	Nugget, Chinook
Hallertauer Mittelfrüh	Lager, bock, wheat	Aroma	Mild and pleasant	Liberty, Saaz, Kent Golding
Kent Golding	All English-style ales, ESB, bitter	Aroma	Gentle and fragrant	Liberty, Hallertauer Mittelfrüh, Mt. Hood

NAME	TYPICAL BEER STYLES	GOOD FOR	SMELL	SUBSTITUTIONS
Liberty	Lager, pilsner, bock, wheat	Aroma	Mild and clean, with a little spice	Hallertauer Mittel-früh, Mt. Hood
Mosaic	Pale ale, IPA	Aroma	Mango, stone fruit, ber-ries, melon	Galaxy, Nelson Sauvin,
Mt. Hood	Lager, pilsner, bock, wheat	Bittering, Aroma	Mild, clean, slightly resinous	Liberty, Hallertauer, Kent Golding
Nelson Sauvin	Pale ale, IPA	Aroma	White wine, grapefruit	Galaxy
Northern Brewer	ESB, bitter, English pale ale, porter	Bittering, Aroma	Wild and earthy	Nugget, Chinook
Nugget	Light lager	Bittering, Aroma	Heavily herbal	Columbus, Chinook, Galena
Saaz	Pilsner	Aroma	Earthy, spicy, herbal	Hallertauer
Simcoe	Pale ale, IPA	Bittering, Aroma	Unique	Citra
Sterling	Lager, ale, pilsner	Aroma	Herbal, spicy, hint of floral and citrus	Saaz
Styrian Golding	All English-style ales, ESB, bitter, lager	Aroma	Delicate, slightly spicy	Fuggle, Willamette
Summit	Pale ale, IPA, stout, porter	Bittering	Orange, tangerine, clementine	Apollo
Warrior	Ale, stout	Bittering	Clean and mellow, mild lemon	Nugget
Willamette	Pale ale, ESB, bitter, English-style ale, porter, stout	Aroma	Fruity, floral, a little earthy	Fuggle, Styrian Golding

in a pelletized form that looks alarmingly like rabbit food. Either way, hops are usually sold in small, labeled packets with the varietal clearly written on the front. You can find them in homebrew shops and some specialty supermarkets, usually kept refrigerated along with the yeast. When you open a packet, you'll get a pungent whiff of that piney, citrusy smell that makes the best IPAs so mouthwatering.

YEAST

These single-celled wonders are the key ingredient in almost all fermented beverages. For beer, you'll want to find a strain of brewer's yeast (*Saccharomyces cerevisiae*). Yeast wranglers (yes, that is the technical term) have identified and cataloged hundreds of different types of yeast tailored to specific styles. But unless you're brewing a Belgian or a sour beer, you can make almost any beer with a simple strain that most brewers call American Ale.

Yeast comes in either dry or liquid form. Dry yeast comes in small packets the size of tea bags. It's best to rehydrate dry yeast in a small amount of water before adding to your beer. Liquid yeast comes in either vials or sealed pouches that should be shaken vigorously before adding to the brew (known as "pitching"), since yeast naturally settles to the bottom. Some of these pouches have a "smack pack" feature—a little bubble inside the packet containing nutrients and a small amount of sugar. When you smack the packet and break the bubble, the liquid nutrients activate the yeast and the packet starts to swell, signaling that the yeast inside is healthy.

Other items you'll need:

- Fermentation vessel
- Siphon
- Hose
- Bung
- Airlock

Optional items:

- Hydrometer
- pH test strips
- Wine thief

THE PROCESS

Now that you have all the essential stuff you'll need, let's walk through a typical extract brewing process. The recipes that follow will help you make specific beers, but here we want to make sure you have a firm handle on what you're doing and why.

The first step is adding water to your pot and bringing it up to around 160°F.

Next, fill a muslin bag with whatever specialty grains you want to use for the recipe. You're essentially making a grain tea bag, which will impart the right combination of flavors for the style. Tie off the end of the muslin bag, and add it straight to the pot. Let that steep for about 30 minutes, then discard the grain bag.

Then heat the liquid to a rolling boil. Stir in the malt extract called for by your specific recipe (liquid or dry), making sure it is fully dissolved. Liquid malt

Common Beer Yeasts

NAME	DESCRIPTION	TYPICAL BEER STYLES	TEMP RANGE (°F)	COMMERCIALLY AVAILABLE STRAINS
American Ale	Clean, crisp flavor with low fruitiness and mild ester production.	IPA, Pale Ale, Stout	60–72	Wyeast 1056; White Labs 001; Safale US-05
British Ale	A rich mineral profile that is bold and crisp. Often used for high gravity ales.	Brown Ale, Porter, Barleywine, Imperial Stout	60–72	Wyeast 1028, 1318; White Labs 002, 013; Safale US-04
European Lager	Perhaps the most widely used lager strain in the world. Produces a distinct malty profile with a crisp finish.	Pilsner, Helles, Märzen	45–68	Wyeast 2124, 2206, 2247-PC, 2278; White Labs 800, 802, 830; Saflager S-23
Irish Ale	Ferments well in dark worts. A good choice for high-gravity beers. Beers fermented in the lower temperature range produce a dry, crisp profile with subtle fruitiness.	Irish Stout, Red Ale, Amber Ale	62–72	Wyeast 1084; White Labs 004; Danstar Windsor
Saison	Produces farmhouse-style ales that are highly aromatic, peppery, spicy, and citrusy. Leaves an unexpected silky and rich mouthfeel.	Saison, Farmhouse Ale, Bière de Garde	70–85	Wyeast 3711, 3724, 3726; White Labs 565, 566; Safbrew T-58
Kölsch	A classic lager/ale hybrid yeast from a traditional brewery in Cologne, Germany. Requires additional settling time to produce bright, clear beers.	Kölsch, American Wheat, Altbier	56–70	Wyeast 2565, 2575-PC; White Labs 029; Safale K-97
Trappist Ale	Widely used and alcohol-tolerant strain. Produces a nice ester profile as well as slightly spicy alcohol notes. It can be slow to start, but ferments well.	Dubbel, Tripel, Belgian Strong	68–78	Wyeast 1214, 3787; White Labs 500, 530, 575
Weizen	Produces a delicate balance of banana and clove flavors. Overpitching can reduce these flavors.	Hefeweizen, Weizenbock	64–75	Wyeast 3056, 3068; White Labs 300, 351, 380; Safbrew WB-06

given the questionable name of *wort* (pronounced "wert"). Boil the wort for a total of about an hour, which will reduce the overall volume of your batch, extract the essential oils from the hops, and concentrate the flavors of the malt. When the boil is done and the volume has reduced by about 30 percent, turn off the heat. If you are brewing an IPA or pale ale and want an extra aromatic kick, you can add some more hops at this point and stir gently for 5 minutes (the pros call this "whirlpool hopping"). Then, you'll need to transfer the pot to an ice bath and cool the wort down to room temperature. This is the most sensitive part of the process—the point at which you could expose the beer to unwanted bacteria or microbes—so try to cool it down as quickly as possible. Be careful to sanitize anything and everything that could come in contact with the wort. (Remember: Always Be Sanitizing!)

tends to settle on the bottom of the pot and scorch into a thick, caramel mess. Dry malt often clumps up into annoying little balls that stubbornly refuse to mix. In either case, steady and patient stirring will eventually lead to an even distribution and save you headaches in the cleanup phase. At this point, you'll have made a sugary solution that smells like a mix of beer and bread.

Next, add hops to the boiling mixture.

Hops added early on in the boiling stage are called bittering hops, since the extended cooking time will release the bitter flavor compounds within. Adding hops toward the end of the boiling stage will lead to less bitterness and more aroma (consult the hop chart for a thorough overview of hop varieties).

The malty, hoppy mixture in your pot is now officially pre-beer, which for some reason has been

Now, it's fermentation time. Pour the contents of the pot into a sanitized bucket or glass carboy. Buckets are much cheaper and easier to clean later, so that's the best vessel for beginners. I prefer glass carboys, though, because you can actually see the fermentation. Use a funnel when pouring wort into a carboy, lest you end up with a mess. At this point, add whatever yeast strain you want to use, and stir to aerate the wort. While air will be your enemy from here on out, yeast needs oxygen to get started, so this is an important step. Close the lid on the bucket or plug the top of the carboy with the stopper. Push the airlock into the stopper hole and make sure it's tight. Whatever airlock you choose, you'll need to

add a little water or sanitizing solution to it to create a closed system.

Set the vessel aside in a cool, dark place for 2 weeks to allow the yeast to do its thing. Bubbles in the airlock will tell you it's working. If you are using a glass carboy, you can watch the magic happen.

The small amount of yeast you added will quickly be fruitful and multiply, forming a 2- to 3-inch layer on the surface called a *krausen*. (As you might expect, there are a lot of German words associated with beer brewing. Later I'll tell you about the *Reinheitsgebot*.)

After 2 weeks, fermentation should be done. If there are still bubbles in your airlock, let it sit until they fade away. Then, transfer the finished beer to another sanitized bucket or pot. Add a small amount of sugar to wake the yeast up again, and stir gently with a sanitized spoon. Bottle the beer in sanitized bottles, cap, and let sit for another 2 weeks while the yeast munches on the extra sugar you gave it. Without an airlock, the CO_2 produced has nowhere to go and dissolves back into the liquid, creating natural carbonation. At this point, you have real, homemade beer.

West Coast IPA

Batch size: 1 gallon

Light lager may be the most ubiquitous beer in the world, but there's no denying that IPA is the most iconic brew these days. Those three letters have become shorthand for a certain kind of beer drinker, an aficionado who scorns the likes of Bud and Coors. These hoppy, aromatic, and very alcoholic concoctions share some common threads but, unlike light lagers, IPAs are not all cut from the same cloth. East Coast versions tend to be lighter in both color and body, while West Coast versions lean on the malt backbone to prop up their hop flavors.

Because of their slight malty sweetness, West Coast IPAs are perfect for extract brewing. Hop varieties from the Pacific Northwest—like Cascade, Centennial, or Chinook—mesh perfectly with the caramel malts that give this beer its distinctive copper color.

INGREDIENTS

1 ounce caramel/crystal malt

Muslin bag for steeping

1½ pounds golden light liquid malt extract

½ ounce Chinook hops (*see* hop chart on page 30 for substitutions)

1 ounce Centennial hops (*see* hop chart on page 30 for substitutions)

1 packet American ale yeast

1 ounce table sugar

INSTRUCTIONS

1. In an 8-quart stockpot, bring 1½ gallons of water to around 160°F. Lightly crush the caramel malt using a mill or the back of a large spoon. Fill the muslin bag with the crushed malt, tie the end, and add to the pot.

2. After about 30 minutes, discard the grain bag and bring the liquid to a rolling boil. Stir in the liquid malt extract, making sure it does not scorch the bottom of the pot. You now have pre-beer, or wort.

Add the Chinook hops and cook for roughly 1 hour, adjusting the temperature so it doesn't boil over.

3. Boil for 60 minutes, reducing the overall volume by about one-third. Turn off the heat and add the Centennial hops. Stir gently for 5 minutes to make sure the hops are evenly distributed throughout the wort, then place the pot in an ice bath and cool to room temperature.

4. When the wort is cooled, transfer the contents of the pot to a sanitized bucket or glass jug. Add the American ale yeast, shake to aerate, and set aside in a cool, dark place for 2 weeks to allow for fermentation.

5. After 2 weeks, siphon the beer out of the fermentation vessel and into a sanitized stockpot. Add the table sugar and stir gently with a sanitized spoon.

6. Bottle the beer in sanitized bottles and let sit at room temperature for another 2 weeks. Chill, open, and enjoy your fully carbonated beer.

Coffee Brown Ale

Batch size: 1 gallon

Coffee and beer are the two most popular beverages in the modern world. And fortunately for those who drink little else (myself included) they go incredibly well together. The creaminess of the crystal malts in this brown ale balances the acidic tannins in the coffee.

The natural oils from coffee can break up the foam "head" on your finished beer, so instead of adding grounds directly to the wort, use pre-brewed coffee. If you want to get fancy with the coffee, paper-filtered methods such as Chemex or AeroPress are preferable to French press or cold brew, since they tend to remove more of the oil.

INGREDIENTS

3 ounces caramel/crystal malt

1 ounce chocolate malt

Muslin bag for steeping

1½ pounds pale liquid malt extract

½ ounce Warrior hops (*see* hop chart on page 30 for substitutions)

1 ounce Willamette hops (*see* hop chart on page 30 for substitutions)

1 cup brewed coffee

1 packet American ale yeast

1 ounce table sugar

INSTRUCTIONS

1. In an 8-quart stockpot, bring 1½ gallons of water to around 160°F. Lightly crush the caramel and chocolate malts using a mill or the back of a large spoon. Fill the muslin bag with the crushed malt, tie the end, and add to the pot.

2. After about 30 minutes, discard the grain bag and bring the liquid to a rolling boil. Stir in the liquid malt extract, making sure it does not scorch the bottom of the pot. You now have pre-beer, or wort. Add the Warrior hops and adjust the temperature so it doesn't boil over.

3. After about 45 minutes, the total volume should be reduced by about one-quarter. Add the Willamette hops and the brewed coffee and cook for another 15 minutes. Turn off the heat, place the pot in an ice bath, and cool to room temperature.

4. Transfer the contents of the pot to a sanitized bucket or glass jug. Add the American ale yeast, shake to aerate, and set aside in a cool, dark place for 2 weeks to allow for fermentation.

5. After 2 weeks, siphon the beer out of the fermentation vessel and into a sanitized stockpot. Add the table sugar and stir gently with a sanitized spoon.

6. Bottle the beer in sanitized bottles and let sit at room temperature for another 2 weeks. Chill, open, and enjoy.

California Common

Batch size: 1 gallon

Also called a "steam beer," this style was made popular by Anchor Brewing Company in San Francisco during the 1980s. With its deep amber color and rich caramel roastiness, it is a close cousin of German Altbier, so using a Kolsch yeast—which is kind of a hybrid between ale and lager—and fermenting around room temperature will give this a distinctly yeasty, estery taste and aroma. Enjoy with a big hunk of good sourdough bread.

INGREDIENTS

4 ounces caramel/crystal malt

Muslin bag for steeping

2 pounds amber dry malt extract

1 ounce Northern Brewer hops (*see* hop chart on page 30 for substitutions)

1 packet Kolsch yeast

1 ounce table sugar

INSTRUCTIONS

1. In an 8-quart stockpot, bring 1½ gallons of water to around 160°F. Lightly crush the caramel malt using a mill or the back of a large spoon. Fill the muslin bag with the crushed malt, tie the end, and add to the pot.

2. After about 30 minutes, discard the grain bag and bring the liquid to a rolling boil. Stir in the dry malt extract powder, making sure all of the clumps are dissolved and the sediment does not scorch the bottom of the pot. You now have pre-beer, or wort. Add half of the Northern Brewer hops and adjust the temperature so it doesn't boil over.

3. After about 45 minutes, the total volume should be reduced by about one-quarter. Add the remaining hops and boil for another 15 minutes, then turn off the heat and place the pot in an ice bath and cool to room temperature.

4. When the wort is cooled, transfer it to a sanitized bucket or glass jug. Add the Kolsch yeast, shake to aerate, and set aside in a cool, dark place for 2 weeks to allow for fermentation.

5. After 2 weeks, siphon the beer out of the fermentation vessel and into a sanitized stockpot. Add the table sugar and stir gently with a sanitized spoon.

6. Bottle the beer in sanitized bottles and let sit at room temperature for another 2 weeks. Chill, open, and enjoy your fully carbonated beer.

Maple Rye Porter

Batch size: 1 gallon

Maple syrup is a completely fermentable sugar, which can be both a good thing and a bad thing. Maple syrup can be used to increase the overall alcohol content or as a substitute for priming sugar at bottling. However, because it's totally fermentable, that rich maple flavor doesn't always make it into the finished beer. To ensure that it shines through, this recipe uses it both ways, as an addition to the fermented wort and as the bottle-conditioning agent. Matched with the spiciness of the rye, this one is so good you'll want to make pancakes with it.

INGREDIENTS

2 ounces chocolate malt

½ ounce black malt

½ ounce rye malt

Muslin bag for steeping

2 pounds amber dry malt extract

1 ounce Fuggle hops (*see* hop chart on page 30 for substitutions)

1 packet British ale yeast

2 ounces maple syrup

INSTRUCTIONS

1. In an 8-quart stockpot, bring 1½ gallons of water to around 160°F. Lightly crush the chocolate, black, and rye malts using a mill or the back of a large wooden spoon. Fill the muslin bag with the crushed malt, tie the end, and add to the pot.

2. After about 30 minutes, discard the grain bag and bring the liquid to a rolling boil. Stir in the dry malt extract powder, making sure all of the clumps are dissolved and the sediment does not scorch the

bottom of the pot. You now have pre-beer, or wort. Add ½ ounce of the Fuggle hops and adjust the temperature so it doesn't boil over.

3. After about 45 minutes, the total volume should be reduced by about one-quarter. Add the remaining ½ ounce of the Fuggle hops and boil for another 15 minutes, then turn off the heat and place the pot in an ice bath and cool to room temperature.

4. When the wort is cooled, transfer the contents of the pot to a sanitized bucket or glass jug. Add the British ale yeast, shake to aerate, and set aside in a cool, dark place.

5. After 1 week, mix 1 ounce of the maple syrup with an equal amount of water and boil. Cool the solution down to room temperature and add it to the beer. Continue fermenting for another week.

6. After 2 weeks, siphon the beer out of the fermentation vessel and into a sanitized stockpot. Add the remaining 1 ounce maple syrup and stir gently with a sanitized spoon.

7. Bottle the beer in sanitized bottles and let sit at room temperature for another 2 weeks. Chill, open, and enjoy.

Winter Warmer

Batch size: 1 gallon

Christmastime in the Great Lakes region can be magical. Snow usually comes early and often, sending sweater-clad Midwesterners bolting for the nearest fireplace. Here in Cleveland, the drink of choice for evenings by the fire is Christmas ale, a spiced concoction rich in both flavor and alcohol. Nearly every local brewery produces Christmas ale by the ton to meet the copious demand, but the most famous version comes from Great Lakes Brewing Company, an early entrant into the Ohio's now-bustling craft brewing scene. This recipe draws inspiration from their beloved brew, but adds a little dark malt to warm it up even more.

INGREDIENTS

2 pounds pale liquid malt extract

4 ounces caramel/crystal malt

1 ounce chocolate malt

½ ounce black malt

Muslin bag for steeping

½ ounce Nugget hops (*see* hop chart on page 30 for substitutions)

¼ teaspoon grated ginger

¼ teaspoon ground cinnamon

¼ teaspoon ground nutmeg

¼ teaspoon ground cloves

1 packet Irish ale yeast

1 ounce table sugar

INSTRUCTIONS

1. In an 8-quart stockpot, bring 1½ gallons of water to around 160°F. Lightly crush the caramel, chocolate, and black malts using a mill or the back of a large spoon. Fill the muslin bag with the crushed malt, tie the end, and add to the pot.

2. After about 30 minutes, discard the grain bag and bring the liquid to a rolling boil. Stir in the liquid malt extract, making sure it does not scorch the bottom of the pot. You now have pre-beer, or wort. Add the Nugget hops and adjust the temperature so it doesn't boil over.

3. Boil for 60 minutes, reducing the volume by about one-third. Turn off the heat and add the ginger, cinnamon, nutmeg, and cloves. Stir gently for 5 minutes, then place the pot in an ice bath and cool to room temperature.

4. When the wort is cooled, transfer it to a sanitized bucket or glass jug. Add the Irish ale yeast, shake to aerate, and set aside in a cool, dark place for 2 weeks to allow for fermentation.

5. After 2 weeks, siphon the beer out of the fermentation vessel and into a sanitized stockpot. Add the table sugar and stir gently with a sanitized spoon.

6. Bottle the beer in sanitized bottles and let sit at room temperature for another 2 weeks. Chill, open, and enjoy your fully carbonated beer.

Bourbon-Barrel Barleywine

Batch size: 1 gallon

While IPAs showcase the diverse flavors you can get from hops, the star of the show in barleywines is malt. Tasting notes for the Platonic ideal of barleywine would feature the words "raisins," "dates," "toffee," and "vanilla." So what would make a better pairing than bourbon?

This recipe simulates barrel aging by adding bourbon-soaked oak chips after the initial fermentation has subsided. Big, high-alcohol beers require a lot of sugar, so this recipe packs as much fermentable goodness into the wort as possible—then adds some more later on in the form of dark brown sugar.

INGREDIENTS

2 ounces Munich malt

3 ounces caramel/crystal malt

1 ounce chocolate malt

Muslin bag for steeping

1 pound pale dry malt extract

1 pound amber dry malt extract

1 ounce Warrior hops (*see* hop chart on page 30 for substitutions)

1 packet American ale yeast

2 ounces dark brown sugar

1 ounce oak chips

1 ounce bourbon

INSTRUCTIONS

1. In an 8-quart stockpot, bring 1½ gallons of water to around 160°F. Lightly crush the Munich, caramel, and chocolate malts using a mill or the back of a large wooden spoon. Fill the muslin bag with the crushed malt, tie the end, and add to the pot.

2. After about 30 minutes, discard the grain bag and bring the liquid to a rolling boil. Stir in the dry malt extract powder, making sure all of the clumps are dissolved and the sediment does not scorch the bottom of the pot. You now have pre-beer, or wort. Add ½ ounce of the Warrior hops and adjust the temperature so it doesn't boil over.

3. After about 45 minutes, the total volume should be reduced by about one-third. Add the remaining ½ ounce of the Warrior hops and boil for another 15 minutes, then turn off the heat and place the pot in an ice bath and cool to room temperature.

4. When the wort is cooled, transfer the contents of the pot to a sanitized bucket or glass jug. Add the yeast, shake to aerate, and set aside in a cool, dark place.

5. After 1 week, mix the dark brown sugar with an equal amount of water and boil. While the solution cools, soak the oak chips in the bourbon. Add the brown sugar and the soaked chips to the beer. Continue fermenting for another week.

6. After 2 weeks, siphon the beer out of the fermentation vessel and into a sanitized stockpot. Add the table sugar and stir gently with a sanitized spoon.

7. Bottle the beer in sanitized bottles and let sit at room temperature for another 2 weeks. For best taste, age the bottles in a cool, dark place for at least 6 months and up to 2 years. Chill, open, and enjoy.

Roasted Pumpkin Stout

Batch size: 1 gallon

There is likely no more divisive style of brew than pumpkin beer.
With their sticky sweetness and cinnamon-and-nutmeg taste, pumpkin beers tend to be viewed either as a luscious confection or an unholy abomination in the eye of the beholder. This recipe aims to split the difference and appeal to both camps. By roasting the pumpkin pieces first, the earthy squash flavor is prominent in the final beer. But the bitter black malts that give stouts their dark complexion help tone down the caramel sweetness and make this more of a meal than a dessert.

Pumpkin beer used to be a seasonal fall treat, but because of its increasing popularity over the past few years, some commercial breweries now start releasing it in July. Maybe cracking one open on a hot afternoon sounds good to you, but personally I'd prefer to hold off until the leaves change. Light a fire and cuddle up with this beer on a cool autumn evening.

INGREDIENTS

3 ounces pumpkin, cubed

2 ounces chocolate malt

1 ounce black malt

Muslin bag for steeping

1½ pounds amber liquid malt extract

½ ounce Warrior hops (*see* hop chart on page 30 for substitutions)

1 ounce Willamette hops (*see* hop chart on page 30 for substitutions)

¼ teaspoon allspice

1 packet British ale yeast

1 ounce dark brown sugar

1 ounce table sugar

INSTRUCTIONS

1. Preheat the oven to 400°F. Cut fresh pumpkin into cubes, and roast for 30 minutes until golden brown. Set aside.

2. In an 8-quart stockpot, bring 1½ gallons of water to around 160°F. Lightly crush the chocolate and black malts using a mill or the back of a large wooden spoon. Fill the muslin bag with the crushed malt, tie the end, and add to the pot.

3. After about 30 minutes, discard the grain bag and bring the liquid to a rolling boil. Stir in the liquid malt extract, making sure it does not scorch the bottom of the pot. You now have pre-beer, or wort. Add the Warrior hops and adjust the temperature so it doesn't boil over.

4. After about 45 minutes, the total volume should be reduced by about one-third. Add the Willamette hops, roasted pumpkin cubes, and allspice and boil for another 15 minutes, then turn off the heat and place the pot in an ice bath and cool to room temperature.

5. When the wort is cooled, transfer the contents of the pot to a sanitized bucket or glass jug, straining out the pumpkin pieces. Add the yeast, shake to aerate, and set aside in a cool, dark place.

6. After 1 week, mix the dark brown sugar with an equal amount of water and boil. Cool the solution down to room temperature and add it to the beer. Continue fermenting for another week.

7. After 2 weeks, siphon the beer out of the fermentation vessel and into a sanitized stockpot. Add the table sugar and stir gently with a sanitized spoon.

8. Bottle the beer in sanitized bottles and let sit at room temperature for another 2 weeks. Chill, open, and enjoy.

The Hard Way

While extract brewing can make a lot of beer with less fuss and minimal investment, if you want to make REALLY good beer, the hard way is the only way. The pure, old-fashioned way. This is what we call *all-grain brewing*. You can set the extract aside for this one, but you'll need everything else from the easy way, plus these items:

GRAIN. LOTS OF IT.

No cheating with sugary syrup this time around. As the name implies, for all-grain brewing you will need to pull the natural sugars out of real grain. The vast majority of this grain will be from a base malt, such as 2-row brewers malt, pale malt, or pilsner malt. The steeping grains you used in the easy way apply here too, supplementing the base malt and determining what style of beer you're brewing.

MASH TUN

This is the big piece of equipment that you can't do without this time around. The mash tun is the vessel you'll use to extract the sugars from the grain and collect the liquid you'll use to make wort. Pretty much any big container made for heat can be a mash tun, but the key is drainage. A stainless steel pot (similar to the brew kettle) with a false bottom and a drainage valve works great, but it can be expensive. Many homebrewers make their own mash tun out of a big Gatorade cooler with some wire mesh on the bottom and a brass ball valve. It sounds intimidating, but it's actually pretty simple to make. There are many excellent YouTube explainer videos for the particulars of DIY construction, depending on the type of cooler you have and the materials you want to use. If you are even remotely handy, I promise you can do it.

Other items you'll need:

- Fermentation vessel
- Siphon
- Hose
- Bung
- Airlock

Optional stuff

- *Grain mill*: You can buy pre-milled grain from a homebrew shop, but if you want to amp up production and keep down costs, buying big sacks of grain and milling it yourself is the way to

Common Grain Malts

NAME	TYPE	DESCRIPTION	TYPICAL BEER STYLES
2-row	Base	Everyday malt that can be used as a base for any beer.	Pale Ale, IPA, Porter, Stout, practically anything
Black Malt	Specialty	Blackened malt that adds intense color and bitterness. Use sparingly.	Stout
Caramel (or Crystal)	Specialty	Malt to be added in small quantities for sweetness. Typically identified by the roasting time (Caramel 60, Caramel 120), which roughly corresponds to sweetness.	Brown Ale
Chocolate	Specialty	Dark roasted malt that adds color and flavor.	Brown Ale, Porter
Golden Naked Oats	Adjunct	A slightly roasted whole oat that adds a sweet berry quality and increased body to the finished beer.	Saison, IPA
Munich	Base, Specialty	A highly kilned base malt that imparts a richer flavor and a deep amber color.	Dunkel, Bock
Maris Otter	Base	A complex and bready malt used in British-style beers and others wanting depth of flavor.	ESB, Pale Ale
Pilsner	Base	Classic malt with a very smooth, clean flavor. Great base malt for many styles.	Lager, Saison, Belgian
Rye	Adjunct	Malted version of the classic grain.	Roggenbier, Rye Ale
Special B	Specialty	Specially roasted for a unique taste. Used almost exclusively in Belgian beers.	Belgian Dubbel and Tripel
Torrified Wheat	Base, Adjunct	A whole-kernel version of flaked wheat. Used to increase head retention and body as an adjunct, but can be the base for certain styles.	Wit, Hefeweizen
Vienna	Base, Specialty	Similar to Munich, but generally a bit lighter due to a shorter kiln time.	Märzen

Grill mill hooked up to a power drill

go. Good grain mills can be expensive, but the money saved on buying in bulk should help subsidize the extra cost.

- *Mash paddle*: Stirring the grain in the mash can be a headache, as pockets of dried grain can ball up and resist penetration of the water. Mash paddles are cheap, effective, and look cool.
- *Heat-resistant hoses*: Draining the wort from the mash tun and transferring it to the kettle is immeasurably easier with heat-resistant silicone hoses (don't bother with the vinyl ones). It avoids spillage and just generally makes things go more smoothly.

THE PROCESS

OK, let's do this.

First, add water to a pot and bring it to around 150°F, the ideal temperature for coaxing sugar out of grain without scalding it. Mill the amount of grain you need for the recipe, and add it into the mash tun.

If you are brewing a recipe that calls for different kinds of malt, make sure they are all evenly distributed throughout the mixture. Then slowly add the water to the mash tun, stirring the grain bed constantly to make sure the water is distributed evenly. This is where the mash paddle comes in handy for stirring to break up any grain balls that might resist taking on water, commonly called *dough balls*. If you don't break up these dough balls early, it will reduce the total sugar you'll be able to draw out from the grain, so mix hard and well. The overall amount of mash water you add at this point will be determined by how much grain you're using and the style of beer you're making.

Let the mash sit for 20 minutes, then stir it again. Repeat stirring after another 20 minutes, and then another. This helps ensure the water is distributed evenly and that any remaining dough balls are broken up. In the meantime, start heating some more water, this time a little hotter, to around 170°F.

Stirring the mash

When an hour has elapsed, drain the liquid from the mash into a bucket or another container. Depending on your setup, as the grain settles the liquid may stop flowing midway through. If this happens, use a spoon or mash paddle to gently stir the grain and ease the flow. Don't stir too hard, though, or the liquid coming out will be thick and full of nasty grain particles. If this happens, you can catch the liquid in a glass or pitcher and pour it back onto the top of the mash until the liquid begins to clear out. This technique is called *vorlauf*. (I told you there would be more fun German words!)

Once all the liquid is drained, check the temperature on your additional water and bring it back up to 170°F, if necessary. The mashed grain still has lots of sugar hanging on to it, so you'll use this extra water to rinse, or *sparge*, the remaining sugar and capture it. There are two ways to sparge: *Fly sparging* requires a garden hose and an intricate fly-wheel adapter to spray the water in a circular manner over the mash at a consistent rate, matching the rate of drainage on the other end. Since I didn't list this piece of equipment above, it probably goes without saying that this is completely impractical for the average brewer. (I like doing things the hard way, but this is absurd.) Instead, *batch sparging* works just as well and is 1,000 times easier. Just add a third of the hot water to the mash, let it sit for 15 min-

utes, and drain into the container with the rest of the mash liquid. Add the next third, and repeat. Same for the final third. That's it. You may experience more drainage problems during the sparge stage, since with the grain moving around, the more dense particles will naturally accumulate at the bottom. This is called a *stuck sparge*, and if it happens, don't worry. Just add a little more water and stir the grain bed again. If that doesn't work, try adding a few handfuls of rice hulls to the mash. You can buy a bag of these long, thin, leaf-like husks at any homebrew shop, and they're handy to have around for just this reason. They won't change the flavor of the brew at all, so add however much you need to get the flow going again.

When you've collected all the liquid from the mash and the sparge, transfer it to the stockpot and bring it to a rolling boil. Add hops for bittering, and now we're right back where we started in the easy way: The malty, hoppy mixture in your pot is now officially wort. Boil for a total of about an hour, then turn off the heat and cool it down to room temperature. Ferment it just as before, and bottle with a bit of priming sugar.

Congratulations, you are now officially a homebrewer.

Session IPA

Batch size: 5 gallons

One of the drawbacks of extract brewing is that it's very difficult to get that beautiful golden body using a syrup or powder as your base. Extracts are prone to scorching during boiling, but even if you use the lightest style and keep a steady, even heat the whole time, at the end your beer will probably still have a copper-colored hue, at best. But with all-grain brewing, you can make blonder beers with ease.

This recipe is for perhaps the most popular style among beer nerds these days: the hoppy session IPA. A modification of the classic pale ale, these beers are at once light and full-bodied, packed with flavor yet totally crushable. On the grain side, the secret is the addition of oats, which along with the wheat helps give this beer a strong mouthfeel without any cloying sweetness.

On the hops side, in keeping with the on-trend theme, this recipe uses an insanely popular New Zealand hop variety called Galaxy, notable for its tropical fruit flavors. You can also use this recipe as a base for showcasing different hop flavors. Try Citra for a citrusy kick (aptly named) or Columbus for a dank, grassy (in more ways than one!) aroma.

INGREDIENTS

8 pounds 2-row malted barley, milled

1 pound golden naked oats

1 pound flaked wheat

3 ounces Galaxy hops (*see* hop chart on page 30 for substitutions)

1 packet ale yeast

5 ounces table sugar

INSTRUCTIONS

1. In a 30-quart stockpot, heat 3 gallons of water to 165°F.

2. Add milled barley, oats, and wheat to your mash tun. Slowly pour the hot water over the grains, stirring constantly to ensure that the water is distributed evenly throughout the grain mixture. Let sit for 1 hour, stirring occasionally.

3. Heat 5 gallons of water to 175°F. Drain the liquid from the mash tun into a separate container. This is your wort. Pour half of the hot water over the grains and let sit for another 15 minutes. Drain the liquid into the container with the rest of the wort, and repeat with the rest of the hot water.

4. When all the wort is collected, transfer back to the stockpot and bring to a rolling boil. Add 1 ounce of the Galaxy hops and cook for 1 hour, until the volume has reduced by about one-third.

5. Turn off the heat and add the remaining 2 ounces of the Galaxy hops. Stir gently for 5 minutes, then place the pot in an ice bath and cool to room temperature.

6. Transfer the contents of the pot to a sanitized bucket or glass carboy with an airlock. Add the yeast, shake to aerate, and set aside in a cool, dark place for 2 weeks to allow for fermentation.

7. After 2 weeks, rack into a container for bottling, add the table sugar and stir gently with a sanitized spoon. Bottle the beer in sanitized bottles and let sit for another 2 weeks. Then open and enjoy your beer.

Bohemian Pilsner

Batch size: 5 gallons

Pilsner is the granddaddy of modern beer. Born in the Czech town of Pilsen in the mid-nineteenth century, this clear, crisp lager spawned thousands of imitations all over the world. Cans of Miller Lite famously boast that it is "a fine Pilsner beer," but those who've sipped a stein in Bohemia know there is no comparison. You can bring that classic Old World taste to your own kitchen with this recipe.

Lagers can be tough to brew at home, as the yeast is much more finicky than its ale cousins. Lager yeast likes lower temperatures, preferably in the high-40s to mid-50s, so you'll need to ferment this either in a dedicated refrigerator set to a warmer-than-normal temperature or a basement. Then they'll need an extra week at room temperature, called a diacetyl rest, to let the yeast munch through some of the by-products of fermentation. Lagers that ferment too warm can taste like buttered popcorn—in a bad way, trust me. But an ideal, cold-fermented pilsner? Well, there's nothing better on a hot summer day.

INGREDIENTS

10 pounds pilsner malt, milled

1 ounce Hallertauer Mittelfrüh hops (*see* hop chart on page 30 for substitutions)

1 ounce Saaz hops (*see* hop chart on page 30 for substitutions)

1 packet European lager yeast

5 ounces table sugar

INSTRUCTIONS

1. In a 30-quart stockpot, heat 3 gallons of water to 165°F.

2. Add milled pilsner malt to your mash tun. Slowly pour the hot water over the grains, stirring constantly to ensure that the water is distributed evenly throughout the grain mixture. Let sit for 1 hour, stirring occasionally.

3. Heat 5 gallons of water to 175°F. Drain the liquid from the mash tun into a separate container. This is your wort. Pour half of the hot water over the grains and let sit for another 15 minutes. Drain the liquid into the container with the rest of the wort, and repeat with the rest of the hot water.

4. When all the wort is collected, transfer back to the stockpot and bring to a rolling boil. Add the Hallertauer Mittelfruh hops and cook for 1 hour, until the volume has reduced by about one-third.

5. Turn off the heat and add the Saaz hops. Stir gently for 5 minutes, then place the pot in an ice bath and cool to room temperature.

6. Transfer the contents of the pot to a sanitized bucket or glass carboy with an airlock. Add the European lager yeast, shake to aerate, and set aside in a cool, dark place, preferably below 60°F, to allow for fermentation.

7. After 2 weeks, rack the beer into another sanitized bucket or carboy and bring up to room temperature. Replace the airlock and let it sit for at least another week.

8. One week later, rack into a container for bottling, add the table sugar, and stir gently with a sanitized spoon. Bottle the beer in sanitized bottles and let sit for another 2 weeks. Then open and enjoy your beer.

Hefeweizen

Batch size: 1 gallon

The original hazy beer, hefeweizen is a cloudy, yeasty wheat brew from Bavaria. Apart from the haze, the wheat gives this beer a strong, full body that serves as a perfect palate for the banana and clove flavors produced by the Weizen yeast. You might see this beer served at bars with an orange slice on the rim, but don't sully the complex flavors here with a needless garnish. Serve it straight up in a tall glass that lets you admire its pillowy white head.

INGREDIENTS

5 pounds pilsner malt, milled

5 pounds torrified red wheat, milled

2 ounces Hallertauer Mittelfruh hops (*see* hop chart on page 30 for substitutions)

1 packet Weizen yeast

5 ounces table sugar

INSTRUCTIONS

1. In a 30-quart stockpot, heat 3 gallons of water to 165°F.

2. Add the milled pilsner malt and torrified red wheat to your mash tun. Slowly pour the hot water over the grains, stirring constantly to ensure that the water is distributed evenly throughout the grain mixture. Let sit for 1 hour, stirring occasionally.

3. Heat 5 gallons of water to 175°F. Drain the liquid from the mash tun into a separate container. This is your wort. Pour half of the hot water over the grains and let sit for another 15 minutes. Drain the

liquid into the container with the rest of the wort, and repeat with the remaining hot water.

4. When all the wort is collected, transfer it back to the stockpot and bring to a rolling boil. Add half of the Hallertauer Mittelfruh hops and cook for 1 hour, until the volume has reduced by about one-third.

5. Turn off the heat and add the remaining hops. Stir gently for 5 minutes, then place the pot in an ice bath and cool to room temperature.

6. Transfer the contents of the pot to a sanitized bucket or glass carboy with an airlock. Add the Weizen yeast, shake to aerate, and set aside in a cool, dark place for 2 weeks to allow for fermentation.

7. After 2 weeks, add the table sugar and stir gently with a sanitized spoon. Bottle the beer in sanitized bottles and let sit for another 2 weeks. Then open and enjoy your beer.

REINHEITSGEBOT: THE GERMAN BEER PURITY LAW OF 1516

In the introduction to this chapter, I said that beer consists of four ingredients—grain, water, hops, and yeast. When I say grain, barley is generally assumed as the predominant variety, although as you can see in these recipes, many other grains can be used. But beer without hops isn't really beer. Is it?

Before the sixteenth century, the notion that hops are an absolutely essential ingredient for beer would have been laughable. Hops were just one of many bitter and aromatic herbs added to beer for better flavor and shelf life. The Ancient Egyptians—yes, they made beer—flavored their brews with za'atar and palm fruit. The Aztecs used cocoa and chili peppers. Romans used hazelnuts and pomegranate seeds. Vikings used birch syrup and bog myrtle. Yum.

Nowadays, we wouldn't call any of those brews "beer," though. They'd be a grain-based gruit (see the recipe for Forest Floor Gruit on page 122). The reason for this is the bureaucratic red tape thrown up by some conservative Bavarian officials in the days when there was still a Holy Roman Empire (which, confusingly, did not include Rome). Wanting to both regulate food safety and help out struggling bakers complaining about the high price of wheat, Duke Wilhelm IV of Bavaria issued the following order:

> "We hereby proclaim and decree, by Authority of our Province, that henceforth in the Duchy of Bavaria, in the country as well as in the cities and marketplaces, the following rules apply to the sale of beer:

> [. . .]

> [I]n all cities, markets and in the country, the only ingredients used for the brewing of beer must be Barley, Hops and Water. Whosoever knowingly disregards or transgresses upon this ordinance, shall be punished by the Court authorities' confiscating such barrels of beer, without fail."[1]

This law became known as the *Reinheitsgebot*, which literally translates to "purity order." You'll likely notice that one of the key four ingredients is missing from this. That's because at the time, science hadn't yet figured out the integral role that yeast plays—nor really even that yeast exists. All brewers knew was if they put new wort into the same vessel that used to hold beer, fermentation would magically happen.

Despite the excessive regulation—or maybe because of it—the Bavarian beer industry flourished. Other kingdoms began to adopt similar ordinances. Brewers from neighboring Bohemia realized the potential of a lightly malted, well-hopped beer, and the Pilsner was born. When Germany was unified in the nineteenth century, the Reinheitsgebot became the law of the land. The rest, as they say, is history.

---

1. Translation by Karl J. Eden in "The History of German Brewing," *Zymurgy Magazine*, Vol. 16, No. 4, 1993.

Dry-Hopped Farmhouse Ale

Batch size: 5 gallons

Saison, grisette, bière de garde— anytime you see those words, know that you're in store for a classic European farmhouse ale. Historically the table beer of peasants in the field, these low-alcohol, high-flavor brews are characterized by a dry, light body and distinctive yeast. Farmhouse ales are the preferred style of a certain sect of nouveau beer geeks.

Classic French and Belgian saisons are highly drinkable, yet subtle and complex. Naturally, when Americans started brewing these beers, we took these delicate flavors and blew them totally out of proportion. Dry-hopping—or adding more hops to the beer after fermentation—is extremely popular with IPA-loving American homebrewers, and it has now crossed over to other styles. The typical American saison is a dry, hoppy concoction that bears only a passing resemblance to its French forebears, but tastes amazing anyway.

INGREDIENTS

10 pounds 2-row malted barley, milled

2 pounds flaked wheat

1 ounce Cluster hops (*see* hop chart on page 30 for substitutions)

5 ounces Nelson Sauvin hops (*see* hop chart on page 30 for substitutions)

1 packet saison yeast

5 ounces table sugar

INSTRUCTIONS

1. In a 30-quart stockpot, heat 3 gallons of water to 165°F.

2. Add milled barley and wheat to your mash tun. Slowly pour the hot water over the grains, stirring constantly to ensure that the water is distributed evenly throughout the grain mixture. Let sit for 1 hour, stirring occasionally.

3. Heat 5 gallons of water to 175°F. Drain the liquid from the mash tun into a separate container. This is your wort. Pour half of the hot water over the grains and let sit for another 15 minutes. Drain the

continued

liquid into the container with the rest of the wort, and repeat with the rest of the hot water.

4. When all the wort is collected, transfer back to the stockpot and bring to a rolling boil. Add the Cluster hops and cook for 1 hour, until the volume has reduced by about one-third.

5. Turn off the heat and add 2 ounces of the Nelson Sauvin hops. Stir gently for 5 minutes, then place the pot in an ice bath and cool to room temperature.

6. Transfer the contents of the pot to a sanitized bucket or glass carboy with an airlock. Add the saison yeast, shake to aerate, and set aside in a cool, dark place for 2 weeks to allow for fermentation.

7. After about a week and a half, when fermentation has subsided, add the remaining 3 ounces of Nelson Sauvin hops directly to the beer. Hops are naturally antimicrobial, so you don't have to worry about contamination.

8. When fermentation is complete, rack into a container for bottling, add the table sugar, and stir gently with a sanitized spoon. Bottle the beer in sanitized bottles and let sit for another 2 weeks. Then open and enjoy.

Hazy Double IPA

Batch size: 5 gallons

Hazy IPA is the hottest trend in craft brewing today. Period.

Inspired by the grandmasters of new-school brewing up in New England—Hill Farmstead, The Alchemist, and Tree House, to name just a few—this massively dry-hopped beer takes the light color, full body, and intense aromas of the Session IPA (see page 54) and literally doubles them. (Well, not quite.) Suitable only for the hoppiest of hop heads, this is a juicy, hazy, flavorful punch in the face.

INGREDIENTS

12 pounds 2-row malted barley, milled

2 pound golden naked oats

2 pound flaked wheat

1 ounce Columbus hops (*see* hop chart on page 30 for substitutions)

2 ounces Citra hops (*see* hop chart on page 30 for substitutions)

1 ounce Amarillo hops (*see* hop chart on page 30 for substitutions)

1 ounce Mosaic hops (*see* hop chart on page 30 for substitutions)

1 ounce Simcoe hops (*see* hop chart on page 30 for substitutions)

1 packet American ale yeast

5 ounces table sugar

INSTRUCTIONS

1. In a 30-quart stockpot, heat 3 gallons of water to 165°F.

2. Add milled barley, oats, and wheat to your mash tun. Slowly pour the hot water over the grains, stirring constantly to ensure that the water is

continued

distributed evenly throughout the grain mixture. Let sit for 1 hour, stirring occasionally.

3. Heat 5 gallons of water to 175°F. Drain the liquid from the mash tun into a separate container. This is your wort. Pour half of the hot water over the grains and let sit for another 15 minutes. Drain the liquid into the container with the rest of the wort, and repeat with the rest of the hot water.

4. When all the wort is collected, transfer back to the stockpot and bring to a rolling boil. Add the Columbus hops and cook for 1 hour, until the volume has reduced by about one-third.

5. Turn off the heat and add the 2 ounces of Citra hops. Stir gently for 5 minutes, then place the pot in an ice bath and cool to room temperature.

6. Transfer the contents of the pot to a sanitized bucket or glass carboy with an airlock. Add the American ale yeast, shake to aerate, and set aside in a cool, dark place for 2 weeks to allow for fermentation.

7. After about a week and a half, when fermentation has subsided, add 1 ounce each of Amarillo, Mosaic, and Simcoe hops directly to the beer. Hops are naturally anti-microbial, so you don't have to worry about contamination.

8. When fermentation is complete, rack into a container for bottling, add the table sugar, and stir gently with a sanitized spoon. Bottle the beer in sanitized bottles and let sit until carbonated. Refrigerate quickly after achieving your desired carbonation level and serve as fresh as possible, as the intense hop flavor and aroma will fade quickly.

Sea Salt Gose

Batch size: 5 gallons

Until a few short years ago, gose was a beer style that seemed lost to history. Like many great beers, it has its roots in a small German village hundreds of years ago. Essentially, gose takes the body of a hefeweizen and then turns it into a salty, sour tonic by letting natural *Lactobacillus* bacteria in the grain take hold during the mash.

Nowadays, gose is a go-to for sour-loving homebrewers who don't want to deal with the headaches and unpredictability that can come from true sour beer making. Instead, you can do what's called *kettle souring*—adding some salt and commercially available lacto mixtures to your wort after the mash and letting it sit overnight. When you boil the next day, you'll have a "clean" beer free of any bacteria, but full of that puckering tartness you crave.

INGREDIENTS

5 pounds pilsner malt, milled

5 pounds torrified red wheat, milled

1 tablespoon sea salt

1 packet *Lactobacillus* culture

1 ounce Cascade hops (*see* hop chart on page 30 for substitutions)

1 packet Weizen yeast

5 ounces table sugar

INSTRUCTIONS

1. In a 30-quart stockpot, heat 3 gallons of water to 165°F.

2. Add milled pilsner malt and wheat to your mash tun. Slowly pour the hot water over the grains, stirring constantly to ensure that the water is distributed evenly throughout the grain mixture. Let sit for 1 hour, stirring occasionally.

3. Heat 5 gallons of water to 175°F. Drain the wort from the mash tun into a separate container. Pour half of the hot water over the grains and let sit for another 15 minutes. Drain the liquid into the

continued

container with the rest of the wort, and repeat with the rest of the hot water.

4. When all the wort is collected, transfer back to the stockpot and let cool to just above room temperature, but no more than 90°F. Add the salt and the *Lactobacillus* culture, cover with foil, and leave on the counter overnight.

5. The following day, uncover the soured wort and bring to a rolling boil. Add the hops and cook for 1 hour, until the volume has reduced by about one-third.

6. Turn off the heat and place the pot in an ice bath and cool to room temperature.

7. Transfer the contents of the pot to a sanitized bucket or glass carboy with an airlock. Add the Weizen yeast, shake to aerate, and set aside in a cool, dark place for 2 weeks to allow for fermentation.

8. After 2 weeks, rack into a container for bottling, add the table sugar, and stir gently with a sanitized spoon. Bottle the beer in sanitized bottles and let sit for another 2 weeks. Then open and enjoy your beer.

Weizenbock

Batch size: 5 gallons

A mash-up of a malty brown bock and a cloudy white hefeweizen, weizenbock is rich and delicate, bready and spicy. Perhaps the most popular example of this style is Schneider Weisse's Aventinus, named for a Bavarian historian from the Renaissance. With its dark fruit flavors, banana and clove overtones, and high alcohol content, weizenbock is a decadent yet refined treat.

INGREDIENTS

6 pounds torrified red wheat, milled

3 pounds pilsner malt, milled

2 pounds Munich malt, milled

2 pounds Vienna malt, milled

1 pound caramel/crystal malt, milled

1 ounce Mt. Hood hops (*see* hop chart on page 30 for substitutions)

1 ounce Saaz hops (*see* hop chart on page 30 for substitutions)

1 packet Weizen yeast

5 ounces table sugar

INSTRUCTIONS

1. In a 30-quart stockpot, heat 3 gallons of water to 165°F.

2. Add the milled wheat, pilsner, Munich, Vienna, and caramel malts to your mash tun. Slowly pour the hot water over the grains, stirring constantly to ensure that the water is distributed evenly throughout the grain mixture. Let sit for 1 hour, stirring occasionally.

continued

3. Heat 5 gallons of water to 175°F. Drain the liquid from the mash tun into a separate container. This is your wort. Pour half of the hot water over the grains and let sit for another 15 minutes. Drain the liquid into the container with the rest of the wort, and repeat with the remaining hot water.

4. When all the wort is collected, transfer it back to the stockpot and bring to a rolling boil. Add the Mt. Hood hops and cook for 1 hour, until the volume has reduced by about one-third.

5. Turn off the heat and add the Saaz hops. Stir gently for 5 minutes, then place the pot in an ice bath and cool to room temperature.

6. Transfer the contents of the pot to a sanitized bucket or glass carboy with an airlock. Add the Weizen yeast, shake to aerate, and set aside in a cool, dark place for 2 weeks to allow for fermentation.

7. After 2 weeks, rack into a container for bottling, add the table sugar, and stir gently with a sanitized spoon. Bottle the beer in sanitized bottles and let sit for another 2 weeks. Then open and enjoy your beer.

Juniper Tripel

Batch size: 5 gallons

A classic Belgian style, *tripel* is the yin to the dark *dubbel*'s yang. Light in color and aroma yet fiercely strong and sweet in body, this beer makes the most of Trappist yeast's faint bubblegum flavors and high alcohol tolerance. All those qualities make this beer a fine canvas for showcasing herbal notes. Adding a few juniper berries at the end of the boil makes this beer taste like a delicious gin cocktail.

INGREDIENTS

10 pounds pilsner malt, milled

1 pound Special B malt, milled

2 pounds torrified red wheat, milled

1 pound flaked wheat

1 pound flaked barley

1 pound light Belgian candy syrup

½ ounce Mt. Hood hops (*see* hop chart on page 30 for substitutions)

1 ounce Kent Golding hops (*see* hop chart on page 30 for substitutions)

1 tablespoon juniper berries

1 packet Trappist ale yeast

5 ounces table sugar

INSTRUCTIONS

1. In a 30-quart stockpot, heat 3 gallons of water to 165°F.

2. Add the milled malts, wheats, and barley to your mash tun. Slowly pour the hot water over the grains, stirring constantly to ensure that the water

continued

is distributed evenly throughout the grain mixture. Let sit for 1 hour, stirring occasionally.

3. Heat 5 gallons of water to 175°F. Drain the liquid from the mash tun into a separate container. This is your wort. Pour half of the hot water over the grains and let sit for another 15 minutes. Drain the liquid into the container with the rest of the wort, and repeat with the remaining hot water.

4. When all the wort is collected, transfer it back to the stockpot and bring to a rolling boil. Add the Mt. Hood hops and cook for 1 hour, until the volume has reduced by about one-third.

5. Turn off the heat and add the Kent Golding hops and juniper berries. Stir gently for 5 minutes, then place the pot in an ice bath and cool to room temperature.

6. Transfer the contents of the pot to a sanitized bucket or glass carboy with an airlock. Add the Trappist yeast, shake to aerate, and set aside in a cool, dark place for 2 weeks to allow for fermentation.

7. After 2 weeks, add the table sugar and stir gently with a sanitized spoon. Bottle the beer in sanitized bottles and let sit for another 2 weeks. Then open and enjoy your beer.

Vanilla Bean Russian Imperial Stout

Batch size: 3 gallons

If pale ales are indie rock, imperial stouts are metal. Like barleywine, imperial stouts are big, alcoholic beasts. They're like regular stouts, but with the volume turned up to 11. (Literally—the recipe below yields roughly an 11 percent alcohol by volume beer. Because of this, note that this recipe only produces 3 gallons.) But unlike other big beers, imperial stouts don't usually push the boundaries of sweetness. The chocolate flavors that emerge from heavily roasted barley offer a counterweight to the sheer tonnage of sugars needed to produce this monstrosity. Add in some pure vanilla bean and you have an indulgent dessert beverage that pairs beautifully with early Black Sabbath.

INGREDIENTS

10 pounds 2-row malted barley, milled

2 pounds chocolate malt, milled

1 pound golden naked oats

1 pound flaked wheat

½ pound caramel malt

2 ounces Chinook hops (*see* hop chart on page 30 for substitutions)

1 packet British ale yeast

1 vanilla bean pod or 1 teaspoon pure vanilla extract

5 ounces table sugar

INSTRUCTIONS

1. In a 30-quart stockpot, heat 2 gallons of water to 165°F.

2. Add the milled barley, chocolate malt, oats, wheat, and caramel malt to your mash tun. Slowly pour the hot water over the grains, stirring constantly to ensure that the water is distributed evenly throughout the grain mixture. Let sit for 1 hour, stirring occasionally.

continued

3. Heat 3 gallons of water to 175°F. Drain the liquid from the mash tun into a separate container. This is your wort. Pour half of the hot water over the grains and let sit for another 15 minutes. Drain the liquid into the container with the rest of the wort, and repeat with the rest of the hot water.

4. When all the wort is collected, transfer back to the stockpot and bring to a rolling boil. Add 1 ounce of the Chinook hops and cook for 1 hour, until the volume has reduced by about one-third.

5. Turn off the heat and add the remaining 1 ounce of Chinook hops. Stir gently for 5 minutes, then place the pot in an ice bath and cool to room temperature.

6. Transfer the contents of the pot to a sanitized bucket or glass carboy with an airlock. Add the British ale yeast, shake to aerate, and set aside in a cool, dark place.

7. After 1 week, add the vanilla bean or vanilla extract.

8. After 2 weeks, rack into a container for bottling, add the table sugar, and stir gently with a sanitized spoon. Bottle the beer in sanitized bottles and let sit for another 2 weeks. Then open and enjoy your beer.

Troubleshooting

WHY ISN'T THE AIRLOCK BUBBLING?

One of the most vexing questions for the novice homebrewer is knowing exactly when fermentation starts. Bubbles in the airlock are the telltale sign, but it can take a few days for this to happen. If you don't see bubbles after 3 or 4 days, it doesn't necessarily mean fermentation isn't happening. Check that you have an airtight seal on your vessel, especially if you're using a bucket with a lid. Next, look for signs of yeast forming on top of the wort (that krausen we talked about earlier). If you don't see krausen and your seal is tight, then the yeast you pitched may not have been healthy. Re-pitch new yeast immediately and wait another day or two. If that doesn't work, try raising the fermentation temperature by 3 to 5 degrees. If none of that works, admit defeat and start over.

WHY DID MY BEER STOP FERMENTING?

Even if you have a healthy fermentation at the beginning of the process, sometimes it doesn't stay that way. If your fermentation stops after only a couple of days, there could be a few reasons why. First, you may have fermented too hot. At high temperatures, yeast tends to burn through its sugar supply very quickly. If so, you may have a beer with some off-flavors (see later questions), but your beer is done fermenting. You may also have underpitched—i.e., not used enough yeast at the start to create a viable colony. Or, if you're brewing a high-alcohol beer like a barleywine or imperial stout, the yeast may not have been able to survive above a certain alcohol threshold. In this case, the solution is to add more yeast.

WHY DID MY FERMENTATION VESSEL OVERFLOW?

When fermentation gets going too quickly or too aggressively, the krausen produced can exceed the headspace in your vessel. Yeasty sludge can start spewing out of the airlock, creating a sticky mess. You can fix this by creating a blowoff tube: Remove the airlock and thread a hose into the opening of the stopper. Place the other end of the hose in a jar filled with sanitizing solution. The krausen will be pushed up the hose and into the jar, not onto your floor.

WHY DOES MY BEER SMELL LIKE NAIL POLISH REMOVER?

If your beer smells like a solvent, you've probably fermented way too hot. High temperatures lead to increased ester production in yeast. Esters are the molecules that can give certain styles their distinctive flavors—like raisin in some dark Belgian beers or banana in some German styles—but run amok these compounds can overwhelm all other flavors. There's no fix for this, unfortunately, so you can either dump the batch or hold your nose and down it.

WHY DOES MY BEER TASTE LIKE BUTTERED POPCORN?

This may not sound like a problem. After all, who doesn't love buttered popcorn? But this buttery or butterscotch flavor isn't very pleasant in the type

of beer it mostly occurs in: pilsner. The cause is an overabundance of a side product of fermentation called diacetyl. Yeast under stress produces excess diacetyl, so beers that have been fermented with weak or underpitched yeast or with insufficient aeration are susceptible to this. Diacetyl is mostly produced early in the fermentation cycle and can dissipate over time. If you encounter this flavor before bottling, let the beer sit in the fermentation vessel at a slightly higher temperature. In lagers, this is known as a diacetyl rest and usually takes care of the problem.

WHY DOES MY BEER SMELL LIKE GRASS?

Some hops can give off a pleasing aroma of freshly cut grass, but if you didn't use one of those and your beer still smells like a lawn mower, you may have a different problem. Malted grains stored with too much moisture can develop a musty smell that transfers to the beer. Similarly, if the hops you use are not properly dried before storage, they can bring some of their garden-esque fragrance to the party. In either case, there's not much you can do to fix the

beer once it's brewed, but try to use better ingredients next time around.

WHY DOES MY BEER TASTE LIKE COUGH SYRUP?

Medicinal flavors in beer can be tough to stomach. Like diacetyl, phenol production during the early stages of fermentation is often the culprit. If you've used a chlorine-based sanitizer, such as bleach, you may have inadvertently encouraged these phenols to proliferate. Using an acid-based sanitizer or rinsing thoroughly with hot water should fix this in your next batch.

WHY IS MY BEER HAZY?

Haziness in homebrew is pretty common, and the cause is usually too slow of a cooling process post-boil. You can accelerate the cooling process by using a wort chiller or counterflow plate, or you can add a teaspoon of Irish moss at the end of the boil to increase clarity. Or you can just embrace the haze. Cloudy beer doesn't really taste different from clear beer, anyway. Just tell your friends it's a wheat beer.

CHAPTER 2

Cider

Many people tend to think of beer as the quintessential American alcoholic beverage. In 2016, the marketing folks at Anheuser-Busch famously (or infamously, depending on whom you ask) rebranded cans of their flagship drink with the word "America" in place of "Budweiser." And in a certain way, it made sense. When we think of blue-collar Americans relaxing with a cold one, in that image the beer is always a domestic lager.

But it wasn't always this way. In the eighteenth and early nineteenth centuries, Americans would have considered themselves cider drinkers first and foremost. When John Chapman, better known as Johnny Appleseed, set out on the Ohio River, his goal wasn't to spread his grandma's apple pie recipe. It was to make sure those salt-of-the-earth frontiersmen had a steady supply of quality fruit for their cider mills. Indeed, as many a historian will tell you, America likely owes its conquest of the West to its love for cider.

Still, cider has always been much more popular in Europe, particularly in France and Spain where *cidre* and *sidra*, respectively, are as cherished as quality white wine. Ciders from the Basque and Normandy regions have long been particularly prized. In the UK, you'll find a less-refined, heavily sweetened version of cider on tap at every corner pub. But in America, it's taken a bit longer to rediscover our roots. During Prohibition, authorities didn't just take an axe to barrels of whiskey. They chopped down many of those cider apple trees that Chapman worked so hard to spread. As a result, America basically lost its cider-making tradition.

That's all changing. Walk into any craft beer bar, and you'll find at least one high-quality cider on the menu. Part of that is due to changing dietary fads; cider is, after all, gluten-free. But it's also a testament to the organic growth of the cider industry in general, as well as the hard work of some truly talented cider-makers.

One of those talented cider-makers is Max Pritchard of Hudson Valley Farmhouse Ciders. I asked him how he got into making cider, and he said it grew out of his food service background. He had been thoroughly schooled in wine while working for Dan Barber at Blue Hill, but found himself drawn to other drinks not traditionally associated with fine dining.

"I was working in restaurants and saw the huge potential for the beverage industry beyond wine," Pritchard told me. "I started to learn more about how the agricultural side can influence the taste—how the grains were grown for beer, how the apples were grown for cider. It was just a natural progression for me to want to understand how cider was made."

Pritchard's wine background hints at a fundamental divide in the American cider scene right now. More traditional cider-makers see their product as closer to wine, like their European counterparts. Steve Wood, who makes New Hampshire's Farnum Hill ciders, plants rare cider apple varieties that make his creations unique and complex. Others, like Andy Brennan of New York's Aaron Burr Cidery, have tried to revive America's natural cider heritage by foraging wild apples.

Some cider-makers, though, look to beer for inspiration. "Reverend Nat up in the Pacific Northwest is doing amazing things," says Pritchard. "He uses cider as a base and adds all kinds of other fruit—watermelon, pineapple, carrots—to make something totally new. Lots of others are adding hops to cider or aging it in bourbon barrels. Kyle Sherrer of Graft makes one that tastes like a gose and sells it in cans."

For aspiring homebrewers who are skittish about trying their first fermentation, though, cider offers another benefit: It is incredibly easy to make. Unlike beer, where you need to coax the sugars out of recalcitrant grains, apples will gladly give up their saccharine payload with a simple squeeze. Hungry yeast will happily devour it too, with virtually no prodding at all. While your beer-brewing friend is still messing with his mash paddle, you'll be sipping on a cool glass of apple alcohol.

But just because it's easier, doesn't mean it's less complex. "A lot of brewers tend to scoff at cider-making," says Pritchard. "It's definitely less labor-intensive, but it's more of an art. Colder, slower fermentations yield better cider than faster fermentations. And you can play around with flavors by mixing different batches together. With beer, you are making a certain style and that is the finished product. With cider, you can mix different base styles and create something new."

The Easy Way

Making cider the easy way essentially consists of moving liquid between various containers and adding a couple of things along the way. That's really it. I'm not kidding. Here's what you'll need.

APPLE CIDER

By far the most important ingredient in making cider is . . . well, cider. The softer kind, also known as "apple juice." The nectar from the ubiquitous apple is the backbone of the dry, effervescent adult beverage you want to make. Just like with other ferments, pretty much any sugary liquid will produce alcohol in the end product, but in terms of flavor it makes a big difference what juice you choose to use.

Most grocery stores carry sweet cider of some form or another. You can often find the crystal-clear, shelf-stable kind in the same aisle as other fruit juices. The cloudier but still pasteurized kind usually lives in a refrigerated area near the produce. The latter is by far the better option of the two, as it carries a bigger flavor punch and can still yield a totally clear product after fermentation.

Given that this method is so simple, though, it may be worth traveling a bit farther to procure your juice. Many local orchards or farmers' markets carry freshly pressed, unpasteurized cider, often using heirloom varietals. If you want to go the full nine yards, you can buy juice directly from orchards

that have a cider-making operation on site. Don't be afraid to ask. You'll be rewarded in the end.

YEAST

As with beer, there are a lot of options for the yeast you can use to ferment. Many yeast labs offer specific strains for cider, but wine or beer yeasts can work just as well and produce interesting flavors. When you're just starting out, the go-to strains are either an English-style cider yeast for a more full-bodied product or a Champagne yeast for a drier, cleaner profile.

PECTIC ENZYME

If you want your cider to be clear, you'll need to add a small amount of this powdered enzyme. Apples naturally contain pectin, a molecule that helps maintain the structure of plant cells. After pressing, the pectin gets redistributed into the juice and starts to bond various compounds together, causing a dis-

Common Cider Yeast Strains		
NAME	DESCRIPTION	TEMPERATURE RANGE (F)
English Cider	Crisp and dry fermenting yeast with a big, fruity finish. Creates a nice balance for all types of apples, pears, and other fruit. Allows fruit character to dominate the profile.	50–70
Champagne	A popular choice for ciders and meads because of its consistently strong fermentation characteristics and high alcohol tolerance, up to 18 percent. Also good for restarting stuck fermentations.	50–80
Premier Cuvee	This Prise de Mousse strain is fast-starting, clean, and neutral. The first choice for champagne and sparkling wines, it makes a great dry cider.	55–75
Cote des Blancs	Cote des Blancs is also known as Epernay II. It imparts a fruity aroma. A slow fermenter, this strain will not ferment to a dryness at the low end of the range—it leaves residual sugar, resulting in a sweeter cider.	50–70
Narbonne	A low-foaming strain that is a very rapid starter and will produce smoother, more aromatic cider that will mature quickly.	50–70
Montrachet	A versatile, all-purpose yeast with complex flavors and aromas. Ferments strongly and has good alcohol tolerance.	50–70

tinct cloudiness. Breaking up the pectin with this enzyme won't really change the flavor of your juice at all, but it makes the cider look a whole lot nicer in the glass.

SULFITES

The big question with any of these fruit-based fermentations is: *To sulfite, or not to sulfite?* Sulfites will kill any naturally occurring yeast or bacteria in your fruit that could affect the flavor during fermenta-

tion. The most common sulfite available is called a Campden tablet, which can be broken up and distributed into your juice 24 hours ahead of fermentation.

The upside of this is quality control and a more complete knowledge of the microbes you're using—though it is worth noting that the naturally occurring yeast and bacteria in healthy fruit are completely harmless. But the downsides of adding sulfites can be significant, too. Some people notice a faint (or not so faint) sulfur smell in the final product, which needless to say is something you'd prefer to avoid. To me, though, the biggest negative is the elimination of potentially interesting flavors. The yeast found on fruit skins can be incredibly diverse. You might stumble on a strain—or a combination of strains—that's impossible to buy commercially or re-create if you tried. The great advantage of home-brewing is experimentation, so why not embrace the unknown?

But yeah, if you prefer to go the safer route, I get it.

Other items you'll need:

- Fermentation vessel
- Siphon
- Hose
- Bung
- Airlock

Optional items:

- Hydrometer
- pH test strips
- Wine thief

THE PROCESS

Now, let's walk through a simple cider-making process. The recipes that follow will help you make specific ciders, but this section will explain more generally what you're doing and why.

First, select the juice you want to use, and bring it to room temperature. Then, pour the juice into the (sanitized!) fermentation vessel of your choice. If you want a clear cider, stir in the pectic enzyme. Add whatever yeast strain you want to use, rehydrating it in a bit of warm water if using dry yeast. Then close the lid on the bucket or plug the top of the carboy with the stopper and an airlock and wait for the magic to begin.

That's pretty much it! Way easier than making beer, right? You get to skip all the boiling and cooling and hopping and proceed right to the fun part: fermentation. Pick a nice, dark spot for your vessel and let the yeast take over. Just like with beer, the fermentation should take about 2 weeks.

When the bubbling in the airlock stops and all of the yeast and cloudiness drops to the bottom, it is best to rack the cider into another clean (and sanitized!) vessel to let the liquid settle out some more. After another week or so in this secondary vessel, you now have a finished still cider. Unlike flat beer, uncarbonated cider is fantastically tasty right out of the fermenter. If you like your cider sans CO_2, then there's nothing left to do but enjoy.

For sparkling cider, transfer the finished cider to another sanitized bucket or pot. Add a small amount of sugar to wake the yeast up again, and stir gently with a sanitized spoon. Bottle the cider in sanitized bottles, cap, and let sit for another 2 weeks while the yeast turns that extra sugar into beautiful bubbles of natural carbonation. Now chill and enjoy your homemade cider.

Simple Cider

Batch size: 1 gallon

A simple, dry cider is both ridicu-lously tasty and ludicrously simple to make. You don't need to get fancy with this one. Use this recipe as a base for your own fermentation experiments down the road.

INGREDIENTS

1 gallon fresh apple cider

1 packet Champagne yeast

1 ounce table sugar

INSTRUCTIONS

1. Pour the cider into a sanitized 1-gallon glass jug.

2. Pour in the Champagne yeast, then place the stopper and airlock on top of the jug. Ferment for 2 weeks.

3. After 2 weeks (or when the airlock stops bubbling), rack the liquid into another cleaned and sanitized glass jug and let it sit for another week.

4. After a week, add the table sugar and 4 ounces of water to a small saucepan and heat until the sugar is dissolved and the solution begins to simmer. Add it to the original jug (which has been cleaned and sanitized) and rack the cider into the jug to combine.

5. Bottle the cider and sugar mixture, cap, and let the bottles naturally carbonate for 2 weeks in a cool, dark place. Chill and enjoy.

Blackberry Cider

Batch size: 1 gallon

Adding fruit to cider can accentuate the flavors and make for a much more interesting brew. But apples are both somewhat subtle and mildly acidic, so you want to use fruits that don't overpower the apple-ness of your drink or turn it cheek-puckeringly astringent. Blackberries are a perfect match for a simple, dry cider.

INGREDIENTS

1 gallon fresh apple cider
½ teaspoon pectic enzyme
1 packet Champagne yeast
½ pint fresh or frozen blackberries
1 ounce table sugar

INSTRUCTIONS

1. Pour the cider into a sanitized 1-gallon glass jug. Add the pectic enzyme and let it sit for 30 minutes.

2. Pitch the yeast, then place the stopper and airlock on top of the jug. Ferment for 2 weeks.

3. After 2 weeks (or when the airlock stops bubbling), add the blackberries to another cleaned and sanitized jug. Rack the cider onto the berries and let it sit for another week.

4. After a week, add the table sugar and 4 ounces of water to a small saucepan and heat until the sugar is dissolved and the solution begins to simmer. Add it to the original jug (which has been cleaned and sanitized) and rack the cider into the jug to combine.

5. Bottle the cider and sugar mixture, cap, and let the bottles naturally carbonate for 2 weeks in a cool, dark place. Chill and enjoy.

Cherry Apple Rosé

Batch size: 1 gallon

Like blackberries, cherries make an ideal companion for apple cider. But unlike their berry cousins, they also impart a rich red color to the final product. Serve this in place of rosé at your next dinner party and I promise you no one will know the difference.

INGREDIENTS

1 gallon fresh apple cider

½ teaspoon pectic enzyme

1 packet Champagne yeast

½ pint fresh or frozen cherries

1 ounce table sugar

INSTRUCTIONS

1. Pour the cider into a sanitized 1-gallon glass jug. Add the pectic enzyme and let it sit for 30 minutes.

2. Pitch the Champagne yeast, then place the stopper and airlock on top of the jug. Ferment for 2 weeks.

3. After 2 weeks (or when the airlock stops bubbling), add the cherries to another cleaned and sanitized jug. Rack the cider onto the cherries and let it sit for another week.

4. After a week, add the table sugar and 4 ounces of water to a small saucepan and heat until the sugar is dissolved and the solution begins to simmer. Add it to the original jug (which has been cleaned and sanitized) and rack the cider into the jug to combine.

5. Bottle the cider and sugar mixture, cap, and let the bottles naturally carbonate for 2 weeks in a cool, dark place. Chill and enjoy.

Ginger & Lemongrass Cider

Batch size: 1 gallon

The spicy bite of ginger and the subtle citrus flavor of lemongrass are a perfect complement for cider.

INGREDIENTS

1 gallon fresh apple cider
1 packet Cote des Blancs yeast
1 ounce freshly grated ginger
2 stalks lemongrass
1 ounce table sugar

INSTRUCTIONS

1. Pour the cider into a sanitized 1-gallon glass jug.

2. Pitch the Champagne yeast, then place the stopper and airlock on top of the jug. Ferment for 2 weeks.

3. After 2 weeks (or when the airlock stops bubbling), add the grated ginger and lemongrass stalks to another cleaned and sanitized jug. Rack the cider onto the ginger and let it sit for another week.

4. After a week, add the table sugar and 4 ounces of water to a small saucepan and heat until the sugar is dissolved and the solution begins to simmer. Add it to the original jug (which has been cleaned and sanitized) and rack the cider into the jug to combine.

5. Bottle the cider and sugar mixture, cap, and let the bottles naturally carbonate for 2 weeks in a cool, dark place. Chill and enjoy.

Basque-Style Sidra

Batch size: 1 gallon

With their distinctive dry, fruity, and almost sour taste, ciders from the Basque region of Spain are world-renowned. You've likely seen photos of this regional specialty being served in its traditionally flamboyant fashion, poured directly from the barrel in an arcing stream or from a bottle held high overhead into a glass at the bartender's waist. The rationale for this is that the sidra needs air to release all of its flavor and aroma, but I can't shake the feeling that it's just for show.

To get these flavors in your own sidra, you'll need some of the region's native yeast. While such yeast is not sold commercially, you can "borrow" it from the bottom of a bottle of good-quality, unfiltered Spanish sidra. Several great labels import to the United States, so ask your local wine shop what they have in stock.

INGREDIENTS

1 gallon fresh apple cider

1 packet Montrachet yeast

Sediment from a bottle of imported Basque cider

INSTRUCTIONS

1. Pour the cider into a sanitized 1-gallon glass jug. Shake gently to aerate the juice.

2. Pitch the Montrachet yeast, then place the stopper and airlock on top of the jug. Ferment for 2 weeks.

3. After 2 weeks (or when the airlock stops bubbling), transfer to another sanitized jug. Add the dregs from the bottle of Basque sidra, and place a new airlock on that vessel. Let the cider mature for at least 1 month and up to 4 months.

4. When the cider is mature, bottle it without any extra sugar. Fermentation should be complete, so the cider will remain still or become only slightly carbonated with age.

The Hard Way

With the easy method, you let the orchard hands do all your dirty work for you. If you want to make cider the real way, you'll need to press the juice yourself. This sounds intimidating, but it's actually pretty rudimentary. The main things you need are:

APPLES

Surprise, surprise—the key ingredient in making quality apple cider is quality apples. When you buy juice commercially, there's no real way to tell what kind of fruit was used to make it. Pressing your own juice gives you complete control over the end product. It's not worth going through all the effort, though, if you're planning to use 100 percent Red Delicious apples from the supermarket. Check out what your local orchard grows, and go from there. The best ciders balance the traits of all the apples used—a little tart, a little sweet, a little bitter, not too acidic. Mix and match various varietals until you hit the combination that speaks to you.

MILL OR FOOD PROCESSOR

Once you have the fruit picked out, it needs to be ground or milled into a slushy mass known as *pomace*. Commercial cideries use a setup that looks like a giant wood chipper and can plow through bushel after bushel of apples at an alarming rate. But for the home cider-maker, really anything that grinds up the apples will do. A ricer or food mill will work, as will a motorized food processor. Use whatever method

you are comfortable with, but keep in mind just how many apples you'll be working with. The bigger the capacity of your grinder or mill, the better.

PRESS

The most important piece of equipment in this process is the press itself, and you really can't do without it. A press applies pressure to your mashed-up fruit and slowly squeezes all of that juicy goodness out of the pulp. You've seen these wood-slatted,

Common Cider Apple Varieties

NAME	APPEARANCE	FLAVOR	SUBSTITUTIONS
Braeburn	Red/orange vertical streaks on a yellow/green background	Balance of sweet and slight tartness	Honeycrisp
Cortland	Red with light streaks of green or yellow and gray/green dots	Sweeter than its cousin McIntosh; adds sugar content to cider	McIntosh, Jonathan
Empire	Bright, shiny red with streaks of yellow	Juicy, firm, and sweet; mix with tart varieties for balance	Honeycrisp, McIntosh
Golden Delicious	Vibrant yellow/green	Very sweet; prone to bruising and discoloration, which can be problematic for cider	Empire
Golden Russet	Brown gold skin	Strong tartness that brings excellent, interesting flavors to cider	Newtown Pippin
Granny Smith	Bright green speckled with white spots	Crisp, tart, and acidic, with a lingering subtle sweetness	Northern Spy
Honeycrisp	Red/orange with splashes of yellow	Good balance of sweet and tart flavors	Empire
Jonathan	Red with areas of green or yellow	Sweet and slightly acidic	McIntosh, Cortland
Kingston Black (also called "Black Taunton")	Deep red with small gray spots	Acidic and tannic; excellent cider apple, though somewhat hard to find	Winesap
McIntosh	Deep red with bright green splotches	Sweet, tart, and very juicy	Jonathan, Cortland
Newtown Pippin	Bright green speckled with brown	Complex, aromatic, and somewhat tart	Golden Russet
Northern Spy	Bright green and deep red in varying designs	Juicy, mildly sweet, and acidic	Granny Smith, Rome
Rome	Bright red with small gray dots	Crisp, juicy, and slightly aromatic	Northern Spy
Winesap	Dark red	Highly aromatic with sweetness and tartness in equal balance	Kingston Black

metal-handled presses before. Undoubtedly, you never thought you'd own one yourself, because it must be expensive. But that's not true! Yes, you can definitely spend hundreds or even thousands of dollars on these if you want to, but you can also find perfectly adequate presses for the home cider-maker for under $200. And it makes sense, because this is not a high-tech piece of machinery. It's a crank and a plate that pushes down on a nylon bag and collects the juice at the bottom. That's really it.

Of course, in some ways, you do get what you pay for. Less expensive presses require a lot of upper body strength and typically are not as structurally sound as some of the more premier models. These fancier presses range from rack-and-cloth models—in which you stack multiple layers of pomace on top of one another with wooden racks in between—to bladder presses. Most bladder presses consist of a perforated metal basin with a rubber bladder that fits in the middle. The pomace is positioned around the edges and water is added slowly to the bladder, so that the displacement pressure from the added liquid pushes the juice through the holes in the basin.

Some homebrew shops will rent out higher-end cider presses for the weekend, which is a good option if you want to give cider-making a try before committing. But if you end up making multiple batches, you are better off just buying your own press or constructing one yourself. The principles behind all presses are fairly intuitive, so the handy weekend warriors among you will be excited by the challenge.

I've been called a lot of things in my life, but "handy" is not one of them. So I happily purchased a less expensive model, and have never looked back.

Can you make cider from apples without a press? Technically, yes. You could transfer your pomace to a wire-mesh strainer lined with cheesecloth and let it drain. Or if you have a commercial juicer, you can collect the liquid through that. But honestly, either one of these methods is a giant pain in the ass and will take approximately 5,000 times longer than using a press. So suck it up and buy one. You'll thank me. I promise.

Other items you'll need:

- Fermentation vessel
- Siphon
- Hose
- Bung
- Airlock

Optional items:

- Hydrometer
- pH test strips
- Wine thief

THE PROCESS

First, select the apples you want to use for your cider. Mix various types of sweet, aromatic, and tart varieties to achieve your desired flavor. Avoid damaged or badly bruised fruit, as it can harbor bacteria or other unwanted microbes, but at the same time, don't

due. Don't use soap or any other chemical sanitizers; just plain old water will do the trick here. When the apples are clean, fill the sink with fresh water and add in your apples for one final quality test. Apples that float are healthy and ready for use. Apples that sink to the bottom should be tossed.

Now it's time to grind. If you are using an industrial-grade mill for this, you don't need to cut up the fruit at all; just drop it in whole. (Also, you are a badass.) But for newbies using a food processor, you'll need to cut the fruit into slightly smaller pieces to get an even grind. Don't grind the fruit too fine, though. You want somewhere between baby food and chunky applesauce. It will look brown and very unappetizing at this point, but don't worry. That's normal.

When you've got the right consistency, collect the pomace into a bucket and keep grinding until all of your apples have become pulp. If you are using multiple apple varieties—which is strongly encouraged—it's worth taking the time to grind and press each one separately. This will allow you to blend the various juices to your taste and give you far greater control in determining the final flavor of your cider.

To juice, add the pomace to the nylon bag inside your press. Position a cleaned and sanitized bucket underneath the press to catch the runoff from the spout. Once it starts flowing, liquid will pour out at a steady clip, so make sure you have another clean bucket handy for when the first fills up. Turn the crank on the press slowly at first, giving the juice

be too much of a stickler for perfect specimens. The apples are all going to end up as pulp anyway.

If you pick the apples fresh, let them sit for a few days after picking. This is referred to as "sweating" the apples, giving them time to further ripen and reduce their overall water content. This may feel like a skippable step, but it can make a huge difference in the quality of the juice. You'll get richer flavors and more concentrated juice. It's worth waiting a day or so even with store-bought apples, too. You'll know when they are ready when you can push lightly and leave a small indentation on the apple, but it still has structural integrity.

Once you're ready to grind, wash the apples thoroughly in cold water to remove any dirt or resi-

time to collect at the bottom before hitting it with more pressure. This will be a slow process and requires patience, lest you leave too much of the juice behind in the fruit. The longer you spend pressing, the greater your juice yield will be.

When you think you've squeezed the pomace dry, open up the press one more time and jostle the apples around. This breaks up any pockets of juice that may have formed within the mash. You can also add a handful of rice hulls to the pomace, which serves the same purpose that it does with stuck sparges in beer brewing.

All told, pressing a bushel of apples is a full day's work. It is labor intensive, physically and mentally taxing, and requires your complete and total attention. But at the end, when you take a sip of your freshly pressed juice, with its subtle and delicate flavors, it will all be worth it.

Store your collected juice overnight at room temperature. Exposed to the air, it will oxidize and quickly turn from a beautiful golden hue to a cloudy brown. This is what you want, though, as it will be a much more stable product. The particles suspended in the juice will settle to the bottom, allowing you to pour off the liquid on top, which is now officially cider. The sweet kind. You can now follow the easy way process to turn it into the hard stuff.

What should you do with the leftover pomace? My initial inclination was just to slop it into the trash, but then I heard about ciderkin. Also called *water-cider* (for reasons that will become obvious), ciderkin is made by adding water back into the spent pomace and pressing it again. The added water pulls out any residual sugars left over from the first press, though the resulting juice is far weaker. Ciderkin typically yields only 2 to 3 percent alcohol by volume, versus anywhere from 7 to 10 percent for straight cider.

Of course, this requires pressing the apple pomace yet again. Perhaps you possess more strength and willpower than most, and for you this sounds like fun. More power to you. I'm just going to go drink my first pressings and be done with it.

Pressed Cider

Batch size: 3 gallons

When you press your own apples, the kind of apples you choose to use is completely up to you. This recipe offers a guide for a blend of varieties that I like and that are easy to find around me in northeast Ohio, but by all means, experiment. Everyone's tastes are different. See what works together for you, and what doesn't.

INSTRUCTIONS

20 pounds of Winesap apples
15 pounds of Golden Russet apples
10 pounds of Jonathan apples
1 packet Champagne yeast
1 ounce table sugar

INSTRUCTIONS

1. Press the entire bushel of apples using your own brute strength. Collect at least 3 gallons of liquid cider and strain out the bits.

2. Pasteurize the juice by heating it in a pot to 160°F. But don't boil it, or the pectin in the apples will add a very unpleasant flavor to the end result.

3. Cool the cider to room temperature and pour it into a sanitized carboy or demijohn, then pour in the Champagne yeast. Place the stopper and air-lock on top of the jug, and ferment.

4. After 2 weeks, rack the cider into another sanitized carboy or demijohn to let it settle.

5. One week later, add the table sugar and 4 ounces of water to a small saucepan and heat until the sugar is dissolved and the solution begins to simmer. Add it to the original fermentation vessel (which has been cleaned and sanitized) and rack the cider to combine.

6. Bottle the cider and sugar mixture, cap, and let the bottles naturally carbonate for 2 weeks in a cool, dark place. Chill and enjoy.

BACKSWEETENING

Traditionally, cider was made dry, with most of the residual sugars fermented out, and the recipes included in this book all follow that method. However, most cider that you buy commercially today has been sweetened after the fact, known as backsweetening. If you've made it this far, though, you know that adding sugar after the fact will just lead to more fermentation. That is, unless you give the yeast a sugar it cannot eat—or simply kill the yeast outright.

For the first method, there are several types of non-fermentable sweeteners you can use. Many of them are usually considered artificial, such as stevia powder, sucralose (Splenda), or aspartame (Sweet'N Low). How much of these to add depends on how sweet you want your cider to be, but I wouldn't recommend using more than a few teaspoons per gallon. Most cider-makers would cringe at adding any of these to a good cider, though, so if you're looking for a more natural substitute, lactose might be the answer. Lactose is sugar derived from dairy, and most yeast strains cannot process it. You'll need to use a bit more for the sweetness to come through, about ½ cup per gallon. Lactose is often used as a sweetening adjunct in beer too, as in milk stouts or cream ales. It does add a distinctly milky flavor, though, so be careful not to use too much. And certainly don't serve it to someone with a dairy allergy!

The second method involves killing the yeast with either additives or heat, then adding the sugar of your choice afterward. Sulfites such as Campden tablets should do the trick, though you may want to also add a yeast inhibitor like potassium sorbate to ensure that fermentation really does stop. Or you can pasteurize the cider by heating it to at least 160°F for 10 minutes. Afterward you can add whatever sugar you want, fermentable or non-fermentable. The purest and best sweetener is more pressed apple juice. If you do that, though, make sure you've pasteurized the additional juice as well, so you're not adding any more natural yeast that could reignite fermenation.

Crabapple Cider

Batch size: 3 gallons

Crabapples are often considered a nuisance.

Crabapple trees generate prodigious amounts of fruit, none of which is remotely palatable for human consumption. Unfermented, that is. When mixed in with a batch of sweeter varieties, these bitter fruits can deliver a complex taste experience that is hard to replicate.

INGREDIENTS

30 pounds of sweet or aromatic apples
10 pounds of crabapples
1 packet Champagne yeast
1 ounce table sugar

INSTRUCTIONS

1. Press the sweet apples and the crabapples together. Collect at least 3 gallons of liquid cider and strain out the bits.

2. Pasteurize the juice by heating it in a pot to 160°F. Do not boil, as it will affect the flavor.

3. Cool the cider to room temperature and pour it into a sanitized carboy or demijohn, then pour in the Champagne yeast. Place the stopper and airlock on top of the jug, and ferment.

4. After 2 weeks, rack the cider into another sanitized carboy or demijohn to let it settle.

5. One week later, add the table sugar and 4 ounces of water to a small saucepan and heat until the sugar is dissolved and the solution begins to simmer. Add it to the original fermentation vessel (which has been cleaned and sanitized) and rack the cider to combine.

6. Bottle the cider and sugar mixture, cap, and let the bottles naturally carbonate for 2 weeks in a cool, dark place. Chill and enjoy.

Perry

Batch size: 3 gallons

Apples aren't the only way to make cider. Pears work just as well but impart their own unique taste. Often called perry, pear cider is hugely popular in the UK and is increasingly gaining traction across the Atlantic.

Since the fruit has a similar texture and consistency to apples, you can use the same grinding and pressing methods to make the juice. Use an English cider yeast to maximize the fruity flavors.

INGREDIENTS

1 bushel of mixed-variety pears (typically 40 pounds)
1 packet English cider yeast
1 ounce table sugar

INSTRUCTIONS

1. Press the entire bushel of pears. Collect at least 3 gallons of liquid perry and strain out the bits.

2. Pasteurize the juice by heating it in a pot to 160°F. Do not boil, as it will affect the flavor.

3. Cool the perry to room temperature and pour it into a sanitized carboy or demijohn, then pour in the English cider yeast. Place the stopper and airlock on top of the jug, and ferment.

4. After 2 weeks, rack the cider into another sanitized carboy or demijohn to let it settle.

5. One week later, add the table sugar and 4 ounces of water to a small saucepan and heat until the sugar is dissolved and the solution begins to simmer. Add it to the original fermentation vessel (which has been cleaned and sanitized) and rack the cider to combine.

6. Bottle the cider and sugar mixture, cap, and let the bottles naturally carbonate for 2 weeks in a cool, dark place. Chill and enjoy.

Applejack Brandy

Batch size: 750 ml

While distilling is beyond the scope of this book, that doesn't mean you can't make high-quality spirits at home. Applejack is traditionally made by leaving a batch of cider outdoors in the winter. As the temperature drops, the water within the cider separates from the alcohol, since the two have different freezing points. When you pour off the liquid from the ice, what's left is a highly alcoholic, highly flavorful brandy.

INGREDIENTS

1 bushel of apples (typically 40 to 45 pounds)
1 packet Champagne yeast
1 ounce table sugar

INSTRUCTIONS

1. Make a batch of pressed cider following the instructions on page 95.

2. When the cider is finished fermenting, transfer the liquid to a sanitized bucket and place it outdoors or in a large chest freezer.

3. When ice forms on the top of the juice, break it up with a sanitized knife or pick. Return it to the cold setting and wait another 24 hours.

4. Pick the ice again and drain the liquid at the bottom into a separate sanitized bucket. Place the collected liquid back in the freezer for another 24 hours.

5. Repeat step 4 again, and then collect the resulting liquid into a sanitized jug. Serve neat.

Cider Saison

Batch size: 5 gallons

One of the great things about
fermentation is that yeast does
not particularly care about purity
of style. As long as you keep it in the right
environment, it will happily chomp through
whatever fermentable sugar you feed it. Sadly,
most brewers don't take advantage of this and
get creative. If the same yeast can make both
beer and cider, why can't it make a hybrid beer/
cider all in one? That's exactly what we'll be
doing here.

INGREDIENTS

10 pounds 2-row malted barley, milled

2 pounds flaked oats

1 ounce Nugget hops

2 ounces Hallertauer Mittelfrüh hops

10 pounds apples (predominantly sweet and aromatic
varieties) or 1 gallon apple juice

1 packet saison yeast

5 ounces table sugar

INSTRUCTIONS

1. In a 30-quart stockpot, heat 2½ gallons of water to 165°F.

2. Add milled barley and oats to your mash tun. Slowly pour the hot water over the grains, stirring constantly to ensure that the water is distributed evenly throughout the grain mixture. Let sit for 1 hour, stirring occasionally.

3. Heat 4 gallons of water to 175°F. Drain the wort from the mash tun into a separate container. Pour half of the hot water over the grains and let sit for another 15 minutes. Drain the liquid into the container with the rest of the wort, and repeat with the rest of the hot water.

4. When all the wort is collected, transfer back to the stockpot and bring to a rolling boil. Add the Nugget hops and cook for 1 hour.

5. Turn off the heat and add the Hallertauer Mittelfrüh hops. Stir gently for 5 minutes, then place the pot in an ice bath and cool to room temperature.

6. While the wort is cooling, grind and press 10 pounds of apples. Collect approximately 1 gallon of juice. (Or, you know, just buy a gallon of juice.) Add the juice to the cooling wort, preferably while the temperature is still above 140°F but no higher than 170°F.

7. Transfer the wort and cider mixture to a sanitized bucket or glass carboy with an airlock. Pitch in the yeast and set aside in a cool, dark place for 2 weeks to allow for fermentation.

8. When fermentation is complete, add the table sugar and stir gently with a sanitized spoon. Bottle your beer/cider hybrid in sanitized bottles and let sit for another 2 weeks. Then open and enjoy.

Troubleshooting

WHY IS MY CIDER CLOUDY?

Like most fruit, apples contain natural pectin that holds its cell walls together. Released during pressing, this pectin can cause a cloudy appearance in the finished cider. Such haziness is totally normal and doesn't really affect the taste. But if you prefer a crystal-clear cider, add a small amount of pectic enzyme before fermentation.

WHY IS THERE A WEIRD FILM ON THE TOP OF MY CIDER?

Cider won't form a noticeable krausen like beer, but if you notice a beige film on the top of your cider, that is probably yeast. However, if your seal isn't airtight or your sanitation wasn't adequate, mold can begin to form on the surface. If so, dump the batch and start over.

WHY DOES MY CIDER TASTE LIKE VINEGAR?

As the name "apple cider vinegar" suggests, over time cider will eventually turn to vinegar. That time frame can be very short or very long, though, depending on the conditions in which you keep your cider. If it is exposed to air for any length of time post-fermentation, your cider is likely to become vinegar quickly. If you don't sanitize properly, same deal. If your cider has turned, unfortunately there's no going back. But thankfully, there are many, many excellent uses for your new batch of all-natural apple cider vinegar! (See Switchel on page 180.)

WHY DOES MY CIDER TASTE LIKE A HAMSTER CAGE?

Lactic acid bacteria—the same stuff used to make gose and other sour beers—can have an odd and unpleasant side effect when applied to cider. This typically happens via cross-contamination from another batch or existing bacteria in the juice itself. It can make the drink taste and smell like a rodent cage, or what folks in the know refer to as "mousy." While it's not at all harmful, very few people like to be reminded of mice in something they intend to drink. Again, there's no way to fix this after the fact, so if you don't like it, try again with better sanitation.

WHY DOES MY CIDER POUR SO SLOWLY?

Certain types of bacteria can turn a cider "ropey" or oily, meaning that it pours like a bottle of Swill from that old *SNL* commercial. These bacteria are not harmful and shouldn't affect the taste or smell of the cider. But if you don't want to drink thick, oily cider, I can't say I blame you.

CHAPTER 3

Mead

When you think of mead, do you think of Vikings? Of strong, solitary heroes boasting of the beasts they've slain, guzzling horn after horn of intoxicating brew? If you polled ten people on the street, how many do you think would be able to say what mead is actually made from? Before picking up this book, would you have known?

Honestly, a lot of people don't. When I bring up mead in conversation, most people think I'm talking about some ancient form of beer. And that's completely understandable. Until the recent buzz around craft beer and artisanal fermented drinks, you'd be forgiven for thinking no one outside of twelfth-century Iceland has touched the stuff.

But in many ways, mead is the simplest alcoholic beverage of them all to make. Like other ferments, it is primarily made from sugar and water, bound up with other flavor compounds unique to its source material. (Which, if you've made it this long in the dark, is honey.) True to its simplicity, mead is most common among societies that can trace their

history back a long time. If you've ever been to an Ethiopian restaurant, the *t'ej* honey wine they serve alongside their shareable platters of stewed meat and vegetables is a highly alcoholic, traditionally flavored mead. Long after they abandoned reaving and plundering, Finns still sip a form of sweet mead called *sima* during their annual May Day festival. More recently on this historical scale, if you've ever been served dandelion wine down South, the base might just be a form of mead.

But the simplicity of the process side doesn't do justice to the complexity of flavors you can get in mead. While it's often spoken of in the same breath as beer or cider, in many ways mead is more like wine. And like wine, the key to making great mead is patience.

I spoke to Jason Kallicragas of the BottleHouse Brewing Company in Cleveland Heights, Ohio, about this point. "Patience is so important with making mead," he said. "The friends I homebrew with, when we make small batches we'll try bottles after 6 months and 9 months and we'll say, 'Eh, it's fine.' Then by month 15 it's excellent and we'll kick ourselves."

Kallicragas started as an assistant brewer for BottleHouse's beer operation, but once he got into brewing mead in his spare time he convinced the owner to let him try making some for their taproom. Now it makes up about 20 percent of their overall sales, and they've started a high-end bottling program. "A lot of first-time mead-makers come from making beer," Kallicragas told me. Craft brewers are notorious for adding all sorts of ancillary things to beer in search of new flavor combinations, and that impulse lends itself well to mead. The strong alcohol base and smooth flavor profile of mead offers a great canvas to build on.

That said, Kallicragas cautions first-timers not to get too crazy too quickly. "If you're starting mead-making, keep your first batches simple. Simple not in the honey-only sense, because I think honey-only meads can be disappointing for first-time brewers. But if you do a fruit mead, don't try to do too much. I see a lot of guys who, in their first batch ever, they add twenty different ingredients. It's hard to learn that way. If it goes wrong, is it wrong because you didn't know how to sanitize a carboy, or is it wrong because the lemon verbena you used shouldn't be fermented that way? Use one or two different things and see how those flavors come through."

Above all, give your mead time to develop. "I've had really nice 7 percent alcohol meads that are bottled, carbonated, and ready to go in less than 6 weeks," says Kallicragas, "but most of the meads I make are wine strength, up to 12 to 14 percent, and I usually age them on the lees for about 6 months to a year." This aging process might seem intimidating, but you really can just put it away and forget about it. Unlike beer or cider, you don't really need to rack mead when you age it. As long as you have a good, airtight seal and minimal headspace, you can leave it in its original vessel for up to a year. And the flavors that develop will be worth the wait.

The Easy Way

Making mead the easy way is extraordinarily similar to making cider. The difference is that you need to make the honey "juice" before you start, but if you've ever made a simple syrup then you know exactly what to do. Here's what you'll need.

HONEY

As the backbone of your mead, sourcing honey is the most important part of the process. Bees are an integral part of the agricultural process, so many of the same farms and orchards that offer interesting

varieties of apples will also carry exceptional honey. Better yet, they'll often have different assortments, based on the type of flowers that the specific hives interacted with most frequently. And they may let you sample them before buying, so you can decide which flavors you want in your mead.

It is worth noting, however, that a lot of the individual character of any particular honey will be lost in fermentation. It's better to tell you this now so you don't get super excited for all the crazy tasting notes in your lavender honey brew. When the yeast chew through all that sugar, they will also devour most of those flavor compounds too, while also giving off their own distinct esters and spice notes.

What is the point of buying good honey if you can't taste it later? Well, let me put it this way: If you use an inferior honey, you will definitely be able to taste it in the end. So buy the good stuff.

YEAST

Many of the same yeast strains you used for beer and cider will work for mead as well. But since mead is by and large much more alcoholic than either of its cousins, you will need a yeast attuned to higher-gravity settings. Wine yeasts work exceptionally well, as do Trappist ale strains.

Other items you'll need:

- Fermentation vessel
- Siphon
- Hose
- Bung
- Airlock

Optional items:

- Hydrometer
- pH test strips
- Wine thief
- Pectic enzyme
- Sulfites

THE PROCESS

Now, let's walk through a simple mead-making process. You'll note that this closely follows the cider-making process.

First, choose your honey. Next, add your honey and your desired amount of water to a saucepan and heat until the mixture is fully dissolved and the temperature reaches at least 150°F but does not exceed 180°F. Turn off the heat and cool to room temperature. Then, pour the honey into the (sanitized!) fermentation vessel of your choice. Add whatever yeast strain you want to use, and close the lid on the bucket or plug the top of the carboy with the stopper and an airlock. Pick a nice, dark spot for your vessel and let the yeast take over. Just like with beer, the fermentation should take about 2 weeks, but the longer you leave it the better it will be.

When the bubbling in the airlock stops and all of the yeast and cloudiness drops to the bottom, you now have mead. Like still cider, uncarbonated mead is a category unto itself. If that's how you like it, then there's nothing left to do but enjoy.

For sparkling mead, transfer the finished mead to another sanitized bucket or pot. Add a little bit more honey to wake the yeast up again, and stir gently with a sanitized spoon. Bottle the mead in sanitized bottles, cap, and let sit for another 2 weeks while the yeast turns that extra sugar into beautiful bubbles of natural carbonation. Chill and enjoy.

Dry Mead

Batch size: 1 gallon

A simple, dry mead is both ridiculously tasty and ludicrously easy to make. It is essentially honey and water, fermented to give it a crisp, boozy bite. You don't need to get fancy with this one. Use this recipe as a base for your own fermentation experiments down the road.

INGREDIENTS

2 pounds honey

1 packet Champagne yeast

1 ounce table sugar

INSTRUCTIONS

1. Pour 2 quarts of water and the honey into a large saucepan, and heat until the honey is fully dissolved. Do not let the temperature exceed 180°F.

2. Cool the mixture to room temperature and transfer to your sanitized fermentation vessel. Add water as necessary until the vessel is mostly full, leaving about 1 inch or so of headspace. Pour in the Champagne yeast, add the stopper and airlock, and ferment until bubbling in the airlock subsides (approximately 2 to 3 weeks).

3. When fermentation is complete, age the mead for at least 4 to 5 weeks or up to a year. Flavors will change and develop over time, so be patient.

4. When you're ready to bottle, add the table sugar to another sanitized container and rack the mead onto the priming sugar so that it is evenly distributed throughout the mead. Bottle and allow 2 weeks for carbonation. Chill and enjoy.

Dandelion Wine

Batch size: 1 gallon

A Southern classic, dandelion wine is often made with simple table sugar, but using honey as the backbone gives it a far more complex flavor. Collect dandelion flowers from your yard as they bloom in the spring, then turn them into this delicious, bittersweet tonic.

INGREDIENTS

2 pounds honey

1 lemon, quartered

1 cup dandelion petals

1 packet Cuvee yeast

1 ounce table sugar

INSTRUCTIONS

1. Pour 2 quarts of water and the honey into a large saucepan, and heat until the honey is fully dissolved and the temperature exceeds 150°F.

2. Pour the hot honey mixture over the lemon and dandelion petals. Cool the mixture to room temperature and transfer to your sanitized fermentation vessel. Add water as necessary until the vessel is mostly full, leaving about 1 inch or so of headspace. Pour in the Cuvee yeast, add the stopper and airlock, and ferment until bubbling in the airlock subsides (approximately 2 to 3 weeks).

3. When fermentation is complete, age the mead for at least 4 to 5 weeks or up to a year. Flavors will change and develop over time, so be patient.

4. When you're ready to bottle, add the table sugar to another sanitized container and rack the mead onto the priming sugar so that it is evenly distributed throughout the mead. Bottle and allow 2 weeks for carbonation. Chill and enjoy.

Black Currant & Fig Melomel

Batch size: 1 gallon

Melomel **is just a fancy word for mead made with fruit.** In this recipe, the currants add a gorgeous deep purple hue. The figs bring a strong fruity nose and a really unique back note on the finish.

INGREDIENTS

2 pounds honey

½ pint black currants

½ pint figs

1 packet Champagne yeast

1 ounce table sugar

INSTRUCTIONS

1. Pour 2 quarts of water and the honey into a large saucepan, and heat until the honey is fully dissolved and the temperature exceeds 150°F.

2. Add the currants and figs to a sanitized 1-gallon glass jug. Pour in the hot honey liquid and let the mixture slowly cool to room temperature. Add water as necessary until the vessel is mostly full, leaving about 1 inch or so of headspace.

3. Pour in the Champagne yeast, add the stopper and airlock, and ferment until bubbling in the airlock subsides (approximately 2 to 3 weeks).

4. When fermentation is complete, age the mead for at least 4 to 5 weeks or up to a year. Flavors will change and develop over time, so be patient.

5. When you're ready to bottle, add the table sugar to another sanitized container and rack the mead onto the priming sugar so that it is evenly distributed throughout the mead. Bottle and allow 2 weeks for carbonation. Chill and enjoy.

Watermelon Mead

Batch size: 1 gallon

Mead offers the perfect base for watermelon fermentations.

The alcohol is strong enough to extract the flavors, but the flavors are subtle enough to let them shine through in the taste. Enjoy this one at a summer barbecue with a generous slice of melon to go with it.

INGREDIENTS

2 pounds honey

1 small watermelon, cubed

1 packet Cote des Blancs yeast

1 ounce table sugar

INSTRUCTIONS

1. Pour 2 quarts of water and the honey into a large saucepan, and heat until the honey is fully dissolved and the temperature exceeds 150°F.

2. Add the cubed watermelon to a sanitized 1-gallon glass jug. Pour in the hot honey liquid and let the mixture slowly cool to room temperature. Add water as necessary until the vessel is mostly full, leaving about 1 inch or so of headspace.

3. Pour in the Cote des Blancs yeast, add the stopper and airlock, and ferment until bubbling in the airlock subsides (approximately 2 to 3 weeks).

4. When fermentation is complete, age the mead for at least 4 to 5 weeks or up to a year. Flavors will change and develop over time, so be patient.

5. When you're ready to bottle, add the table sugar to another sanitized container and rack the mead onto the priming sugar so that it is evenly distributed throughout the mead. Bottle and allow 2 weeks for carbonation. Chill and enjoy.

Apple Pie Mead

Batch size: 1 gallon

There is nothing more classically American than this recipe. Built on a cider base with a touch of honey and fall spice, this one is best enjoyed in the evening by a roaring fire.

INGREDIENTS

1 pound honey

1 teaspoon cinnamon

1 teaspoon nutmeg

¾ gallon sweet apple cider

½ teaspoon pectic enzyme

1 packet Champagne yeast

1 ounce table sugar

INSTRUCTIONS

1. Pour 1 quart of water and the honey into a medium saucepan, and heat until the honey is fully dissolved and the temperature exceeds 150°F.

2. Add the cinnamon and nutmeg to a sanitized 1-gallon glass jug. Pour in the hot honey liquid and let the mixture slowly cool to room temperature.

3. Add the cider and pectic enzyme to the jug, leaving about 1 inch or so of headspace. Pour in the Champagne yeast, add the stopper and airlock, and ferment until bubbling in the airlock subsides (approximately 2 to 3 weeks).

4. When fermentation is complete, add the table sugar to another sanitized container and rack the mead onto the priming sugar. Bottle and allow 2 weeks for carbonation.

The Hard Way

Unless you plan to start your own bee colony in your backyard, there really is no hard way to make mead. As someone who has watched his hand swell up to the size of a softball after a single sting, I'm very comfortable leaving that sort of thing to the professionals. But for those enterprising souls, I would direct you to the excellent book *The New Complete Guide to Beekeeping* by Roger A. Morse (Countryman, 1994).

So if not the bees, what can a seasoned mead-maker do to up their game? Allow the wild into your brew. Harness the power of nature. Embrace the funk.

Wild yeast is all around us. It's in your hair, on tree leaves, floating in the breeze. And crucially, it lives on the skins of fruit and in combs of honey. With a little coaxing and nurturing, you can put it to use for brewing. In short, you can become your own yeast wrangler.

THE PROCESS

There are three distinct ways to culture a wild strain of yeast: from the air, from honey, and from fruit skins. And each one requires its own particular process.

Air: First, create a yeast starter in a small Mason jar with hot water, honey, and yeast nutrient. The jar should be filled a little over two-thirds of the way, leaving a good amount of headspace at the top.

Cover the jar with cheesecloth to prevent insects and other detritus from landing in your mixture. Set the jar next to an open window but away from direct sunlight. It helps if the window is close to your backyard or garden, rather than the street or driveway. Any location with good airflow and a lack of curious critters is best.

After 12 to 24 hours, remove the jar from the window and screw the lid on tight. Shake the jar vigorously to aerate the starter liquid, then unscrew the cap a quarter turn to allow gas to escape. Place the jar in a cool, dark place and let the wild yeast take hold. Within a few days, you should see tiny bubbles climbing up the wall of the jar, indicating the presence of yeast. If you don't see anything yet, don't worry. Since you've likely only captured a small amount of yeast from the air, it can take quite a while for them to multiply to a visible level. Be patient.

One thing you do need to watch out for at this stage is mold. Mold can be quick to form—much quicker than yeast—but it needs an exposed surface to grow. So be sure to give your jar a good shake occasionally until you see evidence of fermentation to discourage mold growth. If you see fuzzy mold, especially brightly colored varieties, toss the batch and start over.

When you have a mold-free and consistently bubbling culture, let the yeast grow until you see visible sediment on the bottom of the jar. Then it's time to pitch it into your bigger batch of brew.

Wild-Cultured Herb Garden Mead

Batch size: 1 gallon

Culture wild yeast and use freshly cut herbs from your own garden for a mead with a true sense of place.

STARTER
3 tablespoons honey

MEAD
2 pounds honey
1 teaspoon sage, chopped
3 sprigs thyme
1 ounce table sugar

INSTRUCTIONS

1. Make a yeast starter by mixing 2 cups of boiling water with 3 tablespoons of honey. Cool it down and transfer to a small Mason jar. Place a cheese-cloth over the jar, secure it with a rubber band, and place it next to an open window or in a backyard garden. Let it sit overnight, then move the jar inside and culture the wild yeast that collected. This should take at least 5 days.

2. When the yeast is fully bloomed, pour 3 quarts of water and 2 pounds of honey into a 10-quart stock-pot, and heat until the honey is fully dissolved and the temperature exceeds 150°F.

3. Let the honey and water mixture cool down to room temperature. Add the sage to a sanitized 1-gallon glass jug along with the sprigs of thyme. Pour in the honey water, leaving at least 2 inches of headspace at the top.

4. Strain out the herbs from the yeast culture and shake to bring the yeast into suspension. Pitch the yeast into the solution, add the stopper and airlock, and ferment until bubbling in the airlock subsides (approximately 2 to 3 weeks).

5. When fermentation is complete, age the mead for at least 4 to 5 weeks or up to a year. Flavors will change and develop over time, so be patient.

6. When you're ready to bottle, add the table sugar to another sanitized container and rack the mead onto the priming sugar so that it is evenly distributed throughout the mead. Bottle and allow 2 weeks for carbonation. Chill and enjoy.

Fruit: Harvesting yeast from fruit is a bit more predictable, but there are still some pitfalls to watch out for. First, select the fruit you want to use. Berries, cherries, or grapes are ideal, since they have tough skins that are natural collecting points for yeast and other (good) microbes. It's better to use fruit that's been grown without the use of chemical pesticides, but microbes are very hardy and can survive even on the most irradiated supermarket produce.

Once you've chosen your fruit, give it a good wash in cold water. Don't worry, the yeast won't go anywhere. Then, make a yeast starter in a small Mason jar as before with hot water, honey, and yeast nutrient. Fill the jar a little over halfway with your cooled starter base, and then add the fruit whole. You don't need to crush up the fruit, since what you're really after are the skins. Screw the lid on tightly, and shake the jar vigorously to make sure the fruit is well covered and the liquid sufficiently aerated. Then unscrew the lid a quarter turn, set the jar in a cool, dark place, and wait.

Because the fruit will float on the surface of the solution, you'll need to be extra vigilant about mold. Shake the solution every few hours to coat any fruit that starts to dry out. Not everything that gathers at the surface will be mold, though. If you start to see large globular bubbles form, connected by thin strands, you may have a *pellicle*. A pellicle is basically a gathering of good bacteria and other microbes that together builds a web of proteins to support itself on the surface of the liquid. Pellicles

A particularly pretty pellicle

look like overlapping ropes or fabric, and you can tell the difference between good bacteria and harmful mold by the bacteria's lack of fuzziness and bright colors. Pellicles can be scary if you've never seen them before, but once you get used to them they'll be a welcome sight. Strains that make some of the most delicious sour beverages in the world—such as *Brettanomyces*, *Lactobacillus*, and *Pediococcus*—

tend to form pellicles, and they are known to grow on many fruit and vegetable skins.

Unless you have captured some particularly strong microbes, though, you should see the signs of wild yeast before any pellicle has time to form.

When you have a thriving microbial culture, let the fermentation continue until you see sediment on the bottom. Then strain out the fruit, stir or shake to bring the yeast back into suspension, and pitch it into your brew.

Blueberry Honey Wine

Batch size: 1 gallon

While blueberries in cider can become lip-puckeringly tart, mead lets their fruity acidity take center stage.

STARTER

3 tablespoons honey
1 pint blueberries

MEAD

2 pounds honey
1 pint blueberries
1 ounce table sugar

INSTRUCTIONS

1. Make a yeast starter by mixing 2 cups of boiling water with 3 tablespoons of honey. Cool it down and add ½ pint of blueberries. Culture the wild yeast from the skins of the blueberries. This should take at least 5 days.

2. When the yeast is fully bloomed, pour 3 quarts of water and 2 pounds of honey into a 10-quart stock-pot, and heat until the honey is fully dissolved and the temperature exceeds 150°F.

3. Let the honey and water mixture cool down to room temperature. Wash the remaining ½ pint of blueberries and add them to a sanitized 1-gallon glass jug. Pour in the honey water, leaving at least 2 inches of headspace at the top.

4. Strain out the berries from the yeast culture and shake to bring the yeast into suspension. Pitch the yeast into the solution, add the stopper and airlock, and ferment until bubbling in the airlock subsides (approximately 2 to 3 weeks).

5. When fermentation is complete, age the mead for at least 4 to 5 weeks or up to a year. Flavors will change and develop over time, so be patient.

6. When you're ready to bottle, add the table sugar to another sanitized container and rack the mead onto the priming sugar so that it is evenly distributed throughout the mead. Bottle and allow 2 weeks for carbonation. Chill and enjoy.

Forest Floor Gruit

Batch size: 1 gallon

As we discussed earlier in relation to the German purity laws, beer made without hops is called *gruit.* There are so many natural bittering and flavoring agents in nature, though, that I promise you won't miss the hoppiness in this one. A mixture of honey and malt extract forms the base, with a mix of herbs from the forest floor rounding out the taste.

STARTER

3 tablespoons honey

1 sprig rosemary

3 mint leaves

MEAD

1 pound honey

1 pound light liquid malt extract

½ pint blackberries

2 sprigs rosemary

1 tablespoon juniper berries

1 ounce table sugar

INSTRUCTIONS

1. Make a yeast starter by mixing 2 cups of boiling water with 3 tablespoons of honey. Cool it down and add the blackberries, 1 sprig of rosemary, and 3 mint leaves. Culture the wild yeast from the surface of the herbs. This should take at least 5 days.

2. When the yeast is fully bloomed, pour 3 quarts of water, 1 pound of honey, and liquid malt extract into a 10-quart stockpot, and heat until the honey and malt are fully dissolved and the temperature exceeds 150°F.

3. Let the mixture cool down to room temperature. Add the remaining 2 sprigs of rosemary and the juniper berries to a sanitized 1-gallon glass jug. Pour in the honey and malt mixture, leaving at least 2 inches of headspace at the top.

4. Strain out the blackberries and herbs from the yeast culture and shake to bring the yeast into suspension. Pitch the yeast into the solution, add the stopper and airlock, and ferment until bubbling in the airlock subsides.

5. When fermentation is complete, rack into another sanitized vessel and leave as little headspace as possible. Age the gruit for up to 6 months. Flavors will change and develop over time, so be patient.

6. When you're ready to bottle, add the table sugar to another sanitized container and rack the gruit onto the priming sugar so that it is evenly distributed throughout. Bottle and allow 2 weeks for carbonation. Chill and enjoy.

Honey: The other way to culture wild yeast is from the honey itself. For this, you will need to use raw honey that has not been pasteurized or heated above 100°F. The best place to find this type of honey is from a farm, orchard, or your weird neighbor who tends his own bee colony.

When you've chosen your honey, simply combine it with cold water in the same ratio as the other starters. This time, fill the jar at least three-quarters of the way to the top, allowing headspace for fermentation but decreasing the amount of air in the jar. Screw the lid on tightly and shake vigorously to combine. Since the water is cold, the honey will fight tenaciously to avoid going into solution, but keep at it. Eventually it will give in, and you'll have a fully mixed and aerated starter. Place the jar in a cool, dark place. Leave the lid screwed tightly, as introducing further air will increase the possibility of turning your honey water into honey vinegar before the yeast has a chance to bloom.

After 24 hours, unscrew the cap and check to see if any pressure is released. If not, stir the mixture lightly with a sanitized spoon and place the lid back on tightly. Check again the next day, and the day after that. Eventually, you will crack the lid and hear a satisfying *whoosh* accompanied by a cascade of bubbles below the surface of the liquid. From then on, check vigilantly for mold while the yeast grows into a full culture. When you see sediment, you're ready to pitch.

Barrel-Aged Wild Cyser

Batch size: 3 gallons

Wood can give an incredibly complex taste to this cider/mead combination. If you don't have access to a barrel, substituting toasted oak chips can accomplish much the same thing. Using cultivated wild yeast dials up the flavor profile even more.

INGREDIENTS

1 bushel of apples (about 40 pounds) or 3 gallons fresh apple cider

6 pounds raw honey

2 packets Champagne yeast

Sediment from your favorite sour beer or wild yeast cultivated from the honey (see previous page)

A used wine or whiskey barrel (or 8 ounces toasted oak chips)

1 ounce table sugar

INSTRUCTIONS

1. Press the entire bushel of apples to collect at least 3 gallons of liquid cider and strain out the bits. (Or, you know, just buy 3 gallons of fresh cider at the grocery store. This one is hard enough already.)

2. Pour the cider into a 20-quart stockpot. Add the honey and heat until fully dissolved. Do not exceed 185°F, or the pectin in the cider will produce off-flavors.

continued

3. Turn off the heat and cool the cider and honey mixture to room temperature. Transfer to a sanitized carboy or demijohn with a stopper and airlock. Pour in the Champagne yeast or cultivated wild yeast and ferment.

4. After 2 weeks, transfer to the barrel (or add the oak chips to your fermentation vessel) and add the dregs from a bottle of your favorite sour beer (or wild yeast you cultivated from the honey). Age the cyser for at least 4 to 5 weeks or up to a year.

Flavors will change and develop over time, so be patient.

5. When you're ready to bottle, add the table sugar to another sanitized container and rack the cyser onto the priming sugar solution so that it is evenly distributed throughout. Bottle and allow at least 2 weeks for carbonation, though it is best to let the bottles condition for several months to allow the flavors to develop. Then chill and enjoy.

Wild Honey Pale Ale

Batch size: 5 gallons

Homebrewers all across America got a little buzz in 2011 when the White House announced that they had started a beer-brewing program at the request of President Barack Obama. That enthusiasm was tempered only slightly when the White House released the recipe for Obama's favorite Honey Ale a year later—an extract rather than all-grain brew. Given all the resources of the federal government at their disposal, many had hoped that America's top chefs would have sprung for the harder way. But you can't accuse them of skimping too much, since they used fresh honey collected from beehives on the White House grounds.

This recipe takes inspiration from our former president, but removes the unnecessary caramel malts from an already sweet brew.

INGREDIENTS

8 pounds 2-row malted barley, milled

1 pound golden naked oats

1 pound flaked wheat

1 ounce Northern Brewer hops

1 ounce Styrian Golding hops

1 pound raw honey

1 packet American ale yeast or cultivated wild yeast

5 ounces table sugar

INSTRUCTIONS

1. In a 30-quart stockpot, heat 3 gallons of water to 165°F.

2. Add milled barley, oats, and wheat to your mash tun. Slowly pour the hot water over the grains, stirring constantly to ensure that the water is distributed evenly throughout the grain mixture. Let sit for 1 hour, stirring occasionally.

3. Heat 5 gallons of water to 175°F. Drain the wort from the mash tun into a separate container. Pour half of the hot water over the grains and let sit for

continued

another 15 minutes. Drain the liquid into the container with the rest of the wort, and repeat with the rest of the hot water.

4. When all the wort is collected, transfer back to the stockpot and bring to a rolling boil. Add the Northern Brewer hops and cook for 1 hour.

5. Add the Styrian Golding hops and the honey and cook for 5 minutes. Turn off the heat and stir gently for 5 more minutes, then place the pot in an ice bath and cool to room temperature.

6. Transfer the contents of the pot to a sanitized bucket or glass carboy with an airlock. Add the yeast and set aside in a cool, dark place for 2 weeks to allow for fermentation.

7. After 2 weeks, add the table sugar and stir gently with a sanitized spoon. Bottle the beer in sanitized bottles and let sit for another 2 weeks. Then open and enjoy your beer.

Troubleshooting

WHY IS MY MEAD STILL SWEET?

Mead can be a much more finicky fermentation than cider or beer, and it can be tough to tell when it's fully done. You can have a steady stream of bubbles for weeks, then taste a sample only to find it's still cloyingly sweet. This is because honey has fewer of the natural yeast nutrients as compared to cider or beer, so halfway through your yeast may just decide to give up. You can head this off by making sure the yeast you use at the start is healthy and active, or you can re-pitch new yeast with some commercially available yeast nutrient solution.

WHY DOES MY MEAD SMELL LIKE EGGS?

Nothing is worse than opening the airlock to your beautiful batch of mead and getting a nose full of rotten eggs. Sulfur compounds are a common by-product of yeast that ferments under stress (i.e., too hot, without key nutrients, or underpitching). This usually happens early on in fermentation, so be patient. If you let it sit these compounds will naturally break down over time and the smell will dissipate. In the future, try to make sure you have healthy, happy yeast at the start to avoid this unpleasantness.

WHY DOES MY MEAD TASTE LIKE VINEGAR?

Like cider, if mead is exposed to air for too long, it will eventually turn to vinegar. Once this happens there is no going back, so take care to ensure that post-fermentation mead is exposed to as little air as possible. Use proper racking techniques and minimize headspace in your fermentation vessel. And if you still end up with vinegar, you can always mix it with some olive oil and make a great salad dressing!

WHY DID MY MEAD TURN BROWN?

As with vinegar, a brown-colored mead is due to overexposure to air (i.e., oxidation). But if the taste is unaffected, you've thankfully avoided losing your entire batch. You can try adding antioxidants such as vitamin C or sulfites, but the color is likely going to stay. In the future, you can avoid this by limiting the amount of headspace you leave in the fermentation vessel and making sure you have an airtight seal.

CHAPTER 4

Sake

I was a seasoned homebrewer before I ever tried to make cider or mead, so when I finally took the plunge it wasn't so hard to learn. After all, the principles and practices are largely the same. When it came to sake, though, I knew I would be in for a challenge.

At its base, sake is simply rice fermented in water, but that's where the simplicity ends. Like the other beverages in this book, it involves creating a sugary medium for yeast to do their work, but extracting the sugars from rice makes things much more complicated. Unlike malted grain, rice will not surrender its sugars to heat alone. It requires the help of a fungus—specifically *Aspergillus oryzae*, known as *koji* in English. A human-friendly type of mold, koji breaks down the complex carbohydrates in the rice slowly, gradually feeding the yeast in a *pas de deux* called parallel fermentation. While this process occurs largely on its own once you get it started, providing all the right conditions for success can be hard work.

The rewards for that effort, though, are well worth it. The ingredients to make sake—rice, koji, yeast, and water—are inexpensive, but the beverage they create is highly prized. Sake is an ancient drink with a rich cultural tradition. Its exact origins are unclear, but alcoholic rice beverages have been made throughout Asia for thousands of years. The first true sake is probably more recent than that—the eighth or ninth century, give or take—but since then it has become the defining drink of Japan. Many consider sake-brewing to be its own art form. If you've seen the documentary *The Birth of Sake* on Netflix, you know how seriously the process is taken by those who make it.

But on this side of the Pacific, there are a few sake brewers trying to kickstart a brand-new American sake culture. I talked to one such brewer in, of all places, Austin, Texas. Jeff Bell, the toji (the sake term for brewmaster) at the Texas

Sake Company, embraces the difference between Japanese and American sake. "When you use American ingredients, it's going to taste different than the Nishiki style rice method. Our sake is more like white wine or sparkling wine."

Bell came to sake via beer. "I used to run Austin Homebrew Supply, and I got into sake making because I wanted to answer people's questions. A lot of people are hyper paranoid about doing it right, and you can't do that without practice, practice, practice."

What attracted Bell to sake, ironically, was the difficulty of the process. "It's the worst of wine, the worst of beer. Wine is one of the easiest products to make, but you have to filter it and adjust the pH and do all that. And then beer you have all this upfront process. Sake is the worst of all that. It takes a week to build up, and then you still have to do all that wine-style filtering at the end."

Bell and other American sake brewers are at the forefront of what they hope will be the next trend in brewing. "Sake is not a market space in America at all. We're creating a niche that will hopefully change the paradigm. Trying to break that idea of only drinking sake with sushi. Sparkling sake is the new thing. We have a cranberry, a dry hopped sake that's almost like an IPA. One thing we're doing is an oak sake, similar to the cedar sake, but ours tastes like a light version of whiskey. Sake is very neutral. Adding flavors into it is the way we're headed now."

The Easy Way

In truth, there is no simple way to make traditional Japanese sake. Making actual sake requires a level of care and attention that I would be remiss to label in any way "easy." However, you can make a rice-based alcoholic beverage that tastes similar and requires much less finesse: sweet rice wine.

The difference between rice wine and sake is not merely a Champagne versus sparkling wine distinction. Beyond the regional nomenclature, there are profound differences in the way the two are made. However, like Champagne and sparkling wine, people continually mix up the two. Try Googling "how to make sake" and you'll be treated to countless YouTube videos that do not, in fact, teach you how to make sake. Many of them are pretty good explainers for this simpler rice wine process, though.

Here's what you'll need:

RICE
Naturally, the key ingredient in rice wine is rice. You'll want to use a starchy rice for this, preferably of the glutinous variety. The best ones to use are the Southeast Asian varieties, like Thai sticky rice.

CHINESE YEAST BALLS
These are also known as "sake balls." I put this in quotes because, again, this is NOT sake. But for some reason, these little balls of yeast, koji, and rice flour are sometimes referred to as sake balls.

You can find these yeast balls in most Asian grocery stores, typically in packs of two golf ball–sized portions.

THE PROCESS

First, wash and cook the rice. In this process, the method of cooking doesn't really matter, though when making actual sake it will matter a great deal. A simple rice cooker is the easiest way, using a 3-to-2 ratio of water to rice. When the rice is finished cooking, cool it down to about room temperature so that it's easy to handle. Next, grind up the yeast balls into a fine powder. Make sure there are no clumps left so that the yeast and koji can be dispersed evenly.

For the fermentation vessel, you'll need something with a large enough opening that you can stick your hand in and reach the bottom. A glass Mason jar or a ceramic crock should work best for smaller batches. For bigger batches, it might be worth making the investment in a carboy with a large, screw-top lid and a pre-drilled hole for the bung and airlock. Because of the difficulty in cleaning carboys and demijohns, these are becoming increasingly common in homebrew shops, with one particular brand marketed under the name Big Mouth Bubbler. They come in both food-grade plastic and glass, but I vastly prefer the glass. You can use these as a vessel for any other fermentation, so if you plan to make both sake and beer, it's definitely worth the money.

Now, start lining your (sanitized!) fermentation vessel with a layer of the cooled rice, about an inch or so thick. Top that off with a sprinkling of the yeast ball powder. Add another layer of rice, followed by another layer of powder. Repeat this until you have all the rice in the jar, but make sure you leave a few inches of headspace at the top.

Place the rice-filled vessel in a cool, dark place and let it ferment. In a few days, you should start to see liquid forming and CO_2 being given off. Depending on the size of the batch and the temperature, it could take anywhere from 2 to 3 weeks to fully ferment. After about a week and a half, start to taste the liquid using a (sanitized!) spoon and stop the process when you hit the right level of flavor and sweetness for your palate. Longer ferments will be drier and perhaps even a little sour.

When you're ready to bottle, pour the mixture through a mesh strainer to catch all the remaining rice and collect the liquid in a clean and sanitized container. The resulting rice wine will be cloudy, but if you let it settle in the refrigerator for a few days it will clear up considerably. Then you can either serve it immediately or rack it and bottle it. If bottling, you'll either want to add sulfites (which could change the flavor) or pasteurize it by submerging the bottles, with just the neck and cap exposed, in a 160°F water bath for 15 minutes. A sous vide machine makes pasteurizing much, much easier—and more precise—so I highly recommend it.

Sorry, Not Sake

Batch size: ½ gallon

This is really a recipe for rice wine, but the Western world seems intent on calling this homebrewed sake. I can't argue that it doesn't taste similar (and delicious in its own right), but I also can't bring myself to call it "sake."

INGREDIENTS
2 pounds sticky rice
2 Chinese yeast balls

INSTRUCTIONS

1. Wash the rice thoroughly with cold water, then add it to a rice cooker or saucepan with 6 cups of water. Cook the rice until the water has completely evaporated and the rice is fluffy and tender.

2. Cool the rice to room temperature, then empty into a clean and sanitized bowl. Grind up the yeast balls with your fingers, and sprinkle the powder over the cooked rice. Stir to make sure the powder is evenly distributed throughout. Transfer to a 1-gallon glass or ceramic jar. Place a layer of cheesecloth over the top of the jar and tighten the lid, then set aside in a cool, dark place.

3. After 1 week, the rice will break down and form a bubbling, opaque liquid. After another few days, smell and taste to check the flavor. Repeat until the desired taste is reached.

4. Before bottling, place a wire mesh strainer and funnel over a 2-quart glass jar, and strain the rice solids from the rice wine mixture. Collect the resulting cloudy white liquid in the jar, and place in the refrigerator overnight.

5. Once the cloudiness has cleared, rack the rice wine into another container. Serve fresh, or bottle and pasteurize.

Lychee "Sake"

Batch size: ½ gallon

Lychee—also spelled liche, lizhi, litchi, or li zhi—is a tropical fruit with a sweet and tart flavor and a pleasingly floral aroma. While not a commonly used fruit in America, you may have read about its supposed health benefits. Or you may have had it in a martini at an Asian fusion restaurant. For the same reason it works in that cocktail, it makes a great addition to any rice wine beverage. The plant is also native to China, so what could be a better addition to a "not-sake" than that?

INGREDIENTS

2 pounds sticky rice
2 Chinese yeast balls
4 to 5 lychee fruit

INSTRUCTIONS

1. Wash the rice thoroughly with cold water, then add it to a rice cooker or saucepan with 6 cups of water. Cook the rice until the water has completely evaporated and the rice is fluffy and tender.

2. Cool the rice to room temperature, then empty into a clean and sanitized bowl. Grind up the yeast balls with your fingers, and sprinkle the powder over the cooked rice. Stir to make sure the powder is evenly distributed throughout. Transfer to a 1-gallon glass or ceramic jar. Place a layer of cheesecloth over the top of the jar and tighten the lid, then set aside in a cool, dark place.

3. After 1 week, the rice will break down and form a bubbling, opaque liquid. After another few days, smell and taste to check the flavor. Repeat until the desired taste is reached.

4. Carefully peel the lychees, remove the pits, and add the fruit to a 3-quart glass. Pour boiling water over the lychees until they are just barely covered, and let the mixture cool back to room temperature. Then, place a wire mesh strainer and funnel over the jar, and pour in the rice wine mixture. Strain the solids and collect the resulting liquid in the jar with the lychee. Place the lid loosely on the jar, and let it sit for 3 to 5 days.

5. After 3 to 5 days, rack the lychee rice wine into a clean container. Let it sit in the refrigerator overnight to clear, then rack into another clean container. Serve fresh, or bottle and pasteurize.

White Peach "Sake"

Batch size: ½ gallon

White peaches tend not to be as sweet as their yellow-hued cousins, and that bite plays well with the flavors in this "sake."

INGREDIENTS

2 pounds sticky rice
2 Chinese yeast balls
1 large white peach, diced

INSTRUCTIONS

1. Wash the rice thoroughly with cold water, then add it to a rice cooker or saucepan with 6 cups of water. Cook the rice until the water has completely evaporated and the rice is fluffy and tender.

2. Cool the rice to room temperature, then empty into a clean and sanitized bowl. Grind up the yeast balls with your fingers, and sprinkle the powder over the cooked rice. Stir to make sure the powder is evenly distributed throughout. Transfer to a 1-gallon glass or ceramic jar. Place a layer of cheesecloth over the top of the jar and tighten the lid, then set aside in a cool, dark place.

3. After 1 week, the rice will break down and form a bubbling, opaque liquid. After another few days, smell and taste to check the flavor. Repeat until the desired taste is reached.

4. Add the diced peach to a 3-quart glass. Pour boiling water over the fruit until it is just barely covered, and let the mixture cool back to room temperature. Then, place a wire mesh strainer and funnel over the jar, and pour in the rice wine mixture. Strain the solids and collect the resulting liquid in the jar with the peaches. Place the lid loosely on the jar, and let it sit for 3 to 5 days.

5. After 3 to 5 days, rack the peach rice wine into a clean container. Let it sit in the refrigerator overnight to clear, then rack into another clean container. Serve fresh, or bottle and pasteurize.

Fuji Apple "Sake"

Batch size: 1 gallon

Cider and "sake" together in one beverage.
This recipe uses Fuji apples—the Red Delicious of Japan—to bring acidity, sweetness, and more fruitiness to the palate.

INGREDIENTS

2 cups sticky rice

2 Chinese yeast balls

10 pounds Fuji apples (or ½ gallon store-bought cider)

INSTRUCTIONS

1. Wash the rice thoroughly with cold water, then add it to a rice cooker or saucepan with 6 cups of water. Cook the rice until the water has completely evaporated and the rice is fluffy and tender.

2. Cool the rice to room temperature, then empty into a clean and sanitized bowl. Grind up the yeast balls with your fingers, and sprinkle the powder over the cooked rice. Stir to make sure the yeast is evenly distributed throughout. Transfer to a 1-gallon glass or ceramic jar. Place a layer of cheesecloth over the top of the jar and tighten the lid, then set aside in a cool, dark place.

3. After 1 week, grind and press 10 pounds of Fuji apples to collect ½ gallon of juice. Pasteurize the juice, and add it to a 1-gallon glass jug. Place a wire mesh strainer and funnel over the jug, and pour in the rice wine mixture, which should still be actively fermenting. Strain the solids and collect the resulting liquid in the jug with the apple juice. Place a bung and airlock on the jug, and let it sit for another 7 to 10 days.

4. When there is no further bubbling in the airlock, rack the apple rice wine into a clean container. Let it sit in the refrigerator overnight to clear, then rack into another clean container. Serve fresh, or bottle and pasteurize.

Sake Bomb Pilsner

Batch size: 5 gallons

If you're not making sake using an orthodox method, why not go all the way and make something truly heretical? Sake bombs are a staple of college-adjacent sushi restaurants all over, and they are made by dropping a glass of sake into a larger glass of beer, preferably a Japanese beer like Kirin or Sapporo. Most Japanese think Americans are nuts for doing this, but that's never stopped us from bastardizing food traditions before.

This recipe captures the essence of the sake bomb in shelf-stable form. It is built off the Bohemian Pilsner recipe on page 56, but with Pacific hops substituted to offend Germans as well.

INGREDIENTS

5 pounds pilsner malt, milled

1 ounce Galaxy hops (*see* hop chart on page 30 for substitutions)

1 ounce Nelson Sauvin hops (*see* hop chart on page 30 for substitutions)

1 packet European lager yeast

2 pounds sticky rice

2 Chinese yeast balls

5 ounces table sugar

INSTRUCTIONS

1. In a 30-quart stockpot, heat 2½ gallons of water to 165°F.

2. Add pilsner malt to your mash tun. Slowly pour the hot water over the grain and let sit for 1 hour, stirring occasionally.

3. Heat 4 gallons of water to 175°F. Drain the wort from the mash tun into a separate container. Pour half of the hot water over the grain and let sit for another 15 minutes. Drain the liquid into the container with the rest of the wort, and repeat with the rest of the hot water.

4. When all the wort is collected, transfer back to the stockpot and bring to a rolling boil. Add the Galaxy hops and cook for 1 hour.

5. Turn off the heat and add the Nelson Sauvin hops. Stir gently for 5 minutes, then place the pot in an ice bath and cool to room temperature.

6. Transfer the contents of the pot to a sanitized bucket or glass carboy with at least 1 gallon's worth of headspace. Pitch the yeast, set the airlock, and place the vessel in a cool, dark place.

7. A few days later, cook the rice in a rice cooker or saucepan with 6 cups of water. Cool the rice to room temperature, then empty into a clean and sanitized bowl. Grind up the yeast balls with your fingers, and sprinkle the powder over the cooked rice. Stir to make sure the powder is evenly distributed throughout. Transfer to a 1-gallon glass or ceramic jar. Place a layer of cheesecloth over the top of the jar and tighten the lid, then set aside in a cool, dark place.

8. After 10 days, place a wire mesh strainer and funnel over a 2-quart glass, and strain the rice solids from the rice wine mixture. Pour the rice wine mixture into the bucket or carboy with the pilsner, which should be mostly fermented at this point. Replace the airlock, and leave for another 4 to 5 days.

9. When there is no further bubbling in the airlock, transfer the sake/beer mixture to another container, add the sugar, and bottle. After 2 weeks of conditioning, open and enjoy.

The Hard Way

Time for the real stuff. Keep it 100. Accept no imitations.

One of the biggest differences between sake and rice wine is that the rice should never touch boiling water. Rice for sake should only be steamed, preferably using a tiered bamboo steamer and a wok for maximum authenticity and street cred. This method also involves growing the koji mold separately, which feels more akin to making cheese than making wine or beer.

Sake is most certainly the hardest fermented beverage to get right, but it is by far the most rewarding when you do. Here's what you'll need.

RICE
This time, you'll want a very specific type of short-grain Japanese rice. There are several different varieties, but the best of these are Yamada Nishiki,

Gohyakumangoku, Miyama Nishiki, and Omachi. There are subtle differences between these strains—so subtle, in fact, that you'd be hard pressed to taste them in your own personal homebrew. Still, this is the main ingredient and the source of most of the flavor in the finished drink, so don't skimp on quality. Use as close to what the pros use as you can find, within reason.

KOJI-KIN
Unlike the combo balls used to make rice wine, real sake requires growing and nurturing a koji rice mixture prior to fermentation. You can order live koji cultures online, but do not use prepackaged, dried koji rice found in some Asian grocery stores. What you need are the spores to grow a live culture yourself. The best place to buy a packet of koji spores is from a specialty retailer online. One company, Vision Brewing, sells this in a small packet that they call a sake homebrew starter kit. Going this route means some extra work, but it is far less expensive than buying a batch of active koji rice. Note that this does not include yeast, which needs to be added later in the process.

YEAST
As with other ferments, a wide variety of yeast strains will work here. But for a more traditional flavor, the best yeasts to use are specifically tailored for making sake. For some arcane reason, special sake yeasts have been assigned a number between 1 and 15. Most of these strains are no longer used, and the

ones most commonly available outside Japan are #7 and #9. When you buy sake yeast from a yeast lab, you're probably getting one of those two.

THE PROCESS

Strap in, this one is going to take awhile.

First, make the koji-kin rice mixture. Measure out about one-third of the total amount of rice you want to use for your sake batch. Soak that rice in water for at least 1 hour, dumping out and changing the water every 20 minutes or so. You want the water to be as clear as possible by the end. At this point the rice will have absorbed a good amount of moisture, and the grains should look almost pearly white.

Steam the presoaked rice for about an hour, making sure that the boiling water never touches the rice. I like to use a tiered bamboo steamer with a moist cloth wrapped around the rice to hold it together. When the rice is done, cool it down until it is still warm to the touch, but not hot.

Sprinkle in the koji-kin spores. Some people recommend mixing the spores with flour or cornstarch to help distribute the granules evenly, but native yeasts and other microbes can live in these, so you'd need to toast the flour before using. This process is already hard enough, so this just seems like self-punishment. I've routinely mixed in koji spores without any flour and it works just fine.

Once the spores are nicely mixed in, move your inoculated rice to a (sanitized!) vessel and keep it at around 90°F for 36 to 48 hours. Yes, unless it's summer and you have no air conditioning, keeping a steady temperature of 90 degrees for that amount of time is not as easy as it sounds. A warm water bath is the easiest way, but make sure no water touches the rice. If you happen to have a sous vide machine (also called an immersion circulator), you can just set the dial and forget it. If you don't, you can keep adding

The oven incubation method

143

Koji rice

warm water intermittently to keep a steady temperature. Or, if you don't want to use your oven for a few days, you can turn it into a makeshift incubator. Just plug in an incandescent work light and place it in the oven along with the koji-inoculated rice and a bowl of water. The worklight will serve as a heat source, and the water will make sure everything stays moist and humid. Every few hours you'll want to shut off the light and open the oven door to make sure it doesn't get too hot. And no matter which incubation method you use,

it's helpful to mix up the rice every 12 hours or so to make sure the culture grows evenly throughout.

After roughly 2 days, you should notice that your rice is now covered with tiny little white hairs and smells faintly cheesy. For those new to mold fermentations, this can be unsettling, to say the least. But don't worry! This is totally and completely normal. You will learn to love that pungent yet pleasant aroma. If you see any black or blue spots on the rice or your rice smells straight-up foul, then something went wrong. Dump the batch immediately. Your nose and eyes will tell you if something is off at this point, but if you've kept the conditions right then there should be no problem.

When you have healthy, thriving koji rice, it's time to make more steamed rice. Soak about half of the remaining premeasured rice, and steam it for about an hour. Cool it down to room temperature and then combine it with half of the koji rice, water, and yeast in a (sanitized!) fermenter. Store the remaining koji rice in a sealed container in the refrigerator; you'll need it again in a few days.

What happens next is called parallel fermentation: The koji will break down the starches in the rice to create sugars, which the yeast will then convert into alcohol and carbon dioxide. The fermentation temperature depends on the preferred conditions for your particular yeast strain, though it's worth noting that I've often gotten the best results by sticking to the lower end of the recommended range.

About 5 to 7 days later, it's time to feed the sake beast once again. Wash, soak, and steam the remaining rice, and pull the koji rice out of the fridge. When the steamed rice is cool and the koji has warmed back up, add them both to the previous mixture along with some extra water. The reason for not adding all the rice and koji at one time is that so much sugar can be a shock to the system, halting that delicately balanced parallel fermentation on one end or the other. Letting this first batch run its course ensures that both the mold and the yeast are healthy and happy, waiting to devour more of the food you give them.

After two more weeks, most of the rice will have broken down into a rather unappealing-looking slurry. Strain out the liquid from the leftover rice (called *lees*) into a separate (sanitized!) container. Just like the rice wine, the cloudy sake will clear up if you let it sit overnight in the refrigerator. If you like it cloudy, though, that's okay too. This type of sake is referred to as nigori.

It's hard to completely get rid of that cloudiness, though. Even the slightest nudge seems to jar some milky white sediment loose, so no matter how many times you rack from one container to another, a bit of whiteness will follow. To get truly clear sake, then, you will need to do some racking or filtering. The latter can be incredibly tedious, as that sediment just does not want to leave on its own. I've tried Brita pitchers, coffee filters, cheesecloth, etc., all with minimal levels of success. Racking offers better results, but still yields a faintly translucent liquid. But at this point, weeks later and aching for a drink, I usually just pour a glass and embrace the nigori.

Junmai Sake

Batch size: 1 gallon

The standard way to make proper sake is often referred to as *junmai.* After fermentation you can decide whether to filter it or serve it *nigori.* This recipe does not call for pasteurization at the end, so technically this would also be referred to as nama.

INGREDIENTS

6 pounds sushi-grade rice
2 tablespoons koji-kin spores
1 packet sake yeast

INSTRUCTIONS

1. Wash 2 pounds of the rice thoroughly in cold water, then soak for at least 1 hour. Drain the rice completely, then transfer to a bamboo steamer and steam for 1 hour.

2. When the rice is cool, spread it out on a clean and sanitized baking sheet. Sprinkle the koji-kin spores over the rice, and mix to ensure even distribution. Collect the koji-inoculated rice into a large Mason jar and place in a warm water bath or incubator at 90°F. Let sit for 36 to 48 hours, mixing the rice every 10 hours to ensure even growth of the koji culture.

3. After 2 days, wash and soak another 2 pounds of rice. Drain and steam the rice for at least 1 hour, then set aside to cool.

4. Combine the cooled steamed rice with half of the koji rice, and place into a 2-gallon bucket or

glass container. Add ½ gallon of water and the full packet of yeast, mix well, and set in a cool, dark place to ferment. Place the remaining koji rice in a sealed container in the refrigerator.

5. After 1 week, wash, soak, and steam the remaining 2 pounds of rice. Cool and combine with the koji rice, and add both to the fermenting sake. Add ½ gallon of water, and let it continue fermenting.

6. After 2 weeks, strain the liquid from the lees, and place the liquid in the refrigerator overnight.

7. For nigori sake, bottle the settled sake directly from this container.

8. For clear sake, rack into another clean container and put it back into the fridge. Do this until most of the sediment is gone, then bottle.

Honjozo Sake

Batch size: 1 gallon

Honjozo **is a style of sake made with a small amount of alcohol added to the mash.** While this addition doesn't noticeably change the overall alcohol content, advocates for this technique say it can add complexity and bring out flavors that you can't get from *junmai*. In my estimation, the differences are very subtle, but it's fun to try new techniques and decide which one you like. Plus, the added alcohol also helps with stability and shelf life. Most traditional sake brewers use alcohol distilled from rice, but you can get the same effect using vodka or gin instead.

INGREDIENTS

6 pounds sushi-grade rice

2 tablespoons koji-kin spores

1 packet sake yeast

3 ounces vodka

INSTRUCTIONS

1. Wash 2 pounds of the rice thoroughly in cold water, then soak for at least 1 hour. Drain the rice completely, then transfer to a bamboo steamer and steam for 1 hour.

2. When the rice is cool, spread it out on a clean and sanitized baking sheet. Sprinkle the koji-kin spores over the rice, and mix to ensure even distribution. Collect the koji-inoculated rice into a large Mason jar and place in a warm water bath or incubator at 90°F. Let sit for 36 to 48 hours, mixing the rice every 10 hours to ensure even growth of the koji culture.

3. After 2 days, wash and soak another 2 pounds of rice. Drain and steam the rice for at least 1 hour, then set aside to cool.

4. Combine the cooled steamed rice with half of the koji rice, and place into a 2-gallon bucket or glass container. Add ½ gallon of water and the full packet of yeast, mix well, and set in a cool, dark place to ferment. Place the remaining koji rice in a sealed container in the refrigerator.

5. After 1 week, wash, soak, and steam the remaining 2 pounds of rice. Cool and combine with the koji rice, and add both to the fermenting sake along with the vodka. Add ½ gallon of water, and let it continue fermenting.

6. After 2 weeks, strain the liquid from the lees, and place the liquid in the refrigerator overnight.

7. For nigori sake, bottle the settled sake directly from this container.

8. For clear sake, rack into another clean container and put it back into the fridge. Do this until most of the sediment is gone, then bottle.

Cedar Sake (Taru)

Batch size: 1 gallon

As oak aging is the defining characteristic of a good Chardonnay, cedar aging is what separates taru from junmai sake. Here we replicate this "aging" process with the addition of a small cedar plank at the end.

INGREDIENTS

6 pounds sushi-grade rice

2 tablespoons koji-kin spores

1 packet sake yeast

1 small cedar plank

INSTRUCTIONS

1. Wash 2 pounds of the rice thoroughly in cold water, then soak for at least 1 hour. Drain the rice completely, then transfer to a bamboo steamer and steam for 1 hour.

2. When the rice is cool, spread it out on a clean and sanitized baking sheet. Sprinkle the koji-kin spores over the rice, and mix to ensure even distribution. Collect the koji-inoculated rice into a large Mason jar and place in a warm water bath or incubator at 90°F. Let sit for 36 to 48 hours, mixing the rice every 10 hours to ensure even growth of the koji culture.

3. After 2 days, wash and soak another 2 pounds of rice. Drain and steam the rice for at least 1 hour, then set aside to cool.

4. Combine the cooled steamed rice with half of the koji rice, and place into a 2-gallon bucket or glass container. Add ½ gallon of water and the full packet of yeast, mix well, and set in a cool, dark place to ferment. Place the remaining koji rice in a sealed container in the refrigerator.

5. After 1 week, wash, soak, and steam the remaining 2 pounds of rice. Cool and combine with the koji rice, and add both to the fermenting sake. Add ½ gallon of water, and let it continue fermenting.

6. After 2 weeks, strain the liquid from the lees, and submerge the cedar plank in the strained liquid. Place the cedar sake in the refrigerator for 3 to 5 days.

7. For nigori sake, bottle the settled sake directly from this container and discard the cedar plank.

8. For clear sake, rack into another clean container and put it back into the fridge with the rinsed cedar plank. Do this until most of the sediment is gone, then bottle.

Shio Koji

Batch size: 1 pint

Now that you are an expert (or at least a learned amateur) at making koji rice, put it to use for making other delicious things in your kitchen. When you prepare your next batch of koji rice for sake, set aside a small amount to mix with salt and water. This will create a medium for pickling meat and vegetables called *shio koji*. Use it to pickle carrots, onions, cucumbers, and daikon radish, or even as a marinade for fish, chicken, or pork.

INGREDIENTS

1 cup koji rice (see process on pages 143–144)
4 tablespoons kosher salt

INSTRUCTIONS

1. Mix the koji rice and salt together in a large bowl. Use your hands to make sure the salt is evenly distributed throughout and the grains of koji rice are broken up as much as possible.

2. Add 1 cup of water and stir. Transfer the mixture to a (sanitized!) pint-sized Mason jar and make sure all the koji grains are submerged. Screw on the lid tightly, then open it a quarter turn to allow for ventilation.

3. Ferment the shio koji mixture at room temperature for at least a week, stirring daily. Add water if the mixture begins to dry out, but don't worry if it starts to thicken. Over time, the saltiness should fade as well.

4. After 1 to 2 weeks, transfer to the refrigerator. You can store it there for up to 6 months. It's best to wait at least 1 month to use for pickling or marinades, to ensure the flavors have matured properly.

Troubleshooting

WHY ISN'T MY KOJI GROWING?

Like other molds, koji can be finicky. It loves warm temperatures, but get it too hot and it won't grow. It needs moisture, but too much liquid and you'll end up with a soggy mess. Growing koji properly requires trial and error. Find the right conditions that work for you. Maybe it's a light-sourced oven. Maybe it's a heating pad. Maybe it's a humid shed in your backyard. Wherever you find success, replicate that process.

WHY IS MY SAKE FOAMING OVER?

Because it's hard to gauge how much fermentable sugar will be created by the koji breaking down the rice, it's common to get an aggressive fermentation from the yeast. If your batch bubbles over, next time leave more headspace for the yeast to do its work.

WHY DOESN'T MY SAKE TASTE LIKE THE ONES FROM JAPAN?

The recipes in this book are for American-style homebrew sake, which is much more flavorful than its intense yet neutral Japanese cousin. You can expect more fruity flavors to come through in the end, and that doesn't mean you've done something wrong.

CHAPTER 5

Kombucha, Kefir & Kvass: Healthy Fermented Drinks & Tonics

There are enough recipes throughout this book to get you good and sauced, so it seems fitting to end on a healthier note. The same fermentation process that fuels all the other alcoholic brews is also behind the nonalcoholic ones. A combination of yeast and bacteria—commonly referred to in health circles as "probiotics"—converts sugars into alcohol but then breaks up the alcohol into other nutritious compounds ready for consumption.

While these probiotic drinks are often referred to as "nonalcoholic," they will naturally retain some traces of alcohol. Not enough to get you buzzed even if you down the whole batch, but present nonetheless. Let's take a closer look at a few of these healthy, nonalcoholic fermented beverages that are easy to make at home.

Kombucha

Kombucha, perhaps the most popular probiotic drink in the world right now, is essentially fermented tea. Kombucha is produced by a SCOBY, or "symbiotic colony of bacteria and yeast." The yeast in this SCOBY, also called a mother, feeds on sugar to create alcohol, which in turn feeds the bacteria that break up the booze into other nutritious compounds. These rubbery, disc-shaped conglomerations will form naturally in sugary beverages if given enough time, just like wild yeast. But you can also buy SCOBYs at health food stores, homebrew shops, or from many online retailers.

The exact health benefits of kombucha are still hotly debated. Many people claim it boosts the human immune response, reduces inflammation from arthritis and rheumatism, and can cure heartburn, hypertension, diabetes, and even cancer. While the jury is still out on most of that, the general consensus is that, like most probiotic drinks, kombucha greatly aids digestion. By replacing and supplementing the so-called "gut flora" that the modern diet tends to repress, the microbes in kombucha can aid people suffering from constipation, diarrhea, and irritable bowel syndrome.

Me? I just like the taste. Like the best sour beers, kombucha has a terrific balance of sweet, tart, and savory, thanks to its blend of tea, sugar, and fermentables. It is also a fantastic medium for fruit ferments, which can bring all kinds of different flavors to the fore.

Sour Lemon Earl Grey Kombucha

Batch size: 1 gallon

A strong and lemony black tea makes the perfect base for this entry-level kombucha. A squeeze of lemon juice and some zest perks this healthy drink up even more. Note that when you make your first batch of kombucha, it is important to add a little of the store-bought stuff to ensure the right pH and nutrients for your SCOBY to grow and multiply. Every time after, you can just add a little bit from your previous batch into the new one to get the same effect.

INGREDIENTS

1 cup table sugar

8 bags Earl Grey tea

1 lemon, juiced and peeled

2 cups kombucha from previous batch (or unpasteurized store-bought kombucha)

1 SCOBY per fermentation jar

INSTRUCTIONS

1. Boil 1 gallon of water and stir in the sugar to dissolve. Add the tea bags and let the tea steep for at least 30 minutes, then add the lemon juice and lemon peel. Cool the tea in an ice bath to bring it to room temperature.

2. Once the tea is cool, remove the tea bags and stir in the starter kombucha. Pour the mixture into a 1-gallon glass jar and gently slide the SCOBY into the jar with clean hands. Cover the mouth of the jar with cheesecloth and secure it with a rubber band.

3. Keep the jar at room temperature, out of direct sunlight, and let it ferment for a week to 10 days. Check the jar periodically. A new SCOBY should start forming on the surface of the kombucha within a few days, usually attached to the old one. You might be unsettled by the sight of sediment and other random junk floating around in the jar, but this is all totally normal. Kombucha is a living thing.

4. After about a week, begin tasting the kombucha every day by pouring a little out of the jar. When it

continued

reaches a balance of sweetness and tartness that works for you, it's time to bottle. Before you bottle, get your next batch of kombucha ready, following the same steps as above. Remove the SCOBY and add it to the new batch.

5. Measure out your starter tea from this batch of kombucha to use next time. Pour the fermented kombucha into bottles. Leave about an inch of headspace in each bottle.

6. Store the bottled kombucha in a cool, dark place to carbonate. It should take about 3 or 4 days. Put the bottles in the refrigerator to stop fermentation. Your kombucha should last about a month or so.

Mixed Berry Chamomile Kombucha

Batch size: 1 gallon

Chamomile has long been the go-to herbal tea for days when you are under the weather. Putting it in kombucha form adds the benefits of pro-biotics, and including berries makes the whole thing a little bit sweeter. Note that a bit of black tea is still necessary to maintain the health of the SCOBY, but not enough to affect the flavor very much.

INGREDIENTS

1 cup table sugar

6 bags chamomile tea

2 bags black tea

½ pint strawberries, chopped

½ pint blackberries, chopped

2 cups kombucha from previous batch (or unpasteurized store-bought kombucha)

1 SCOBY per fermentation jar

continued

INSTRUCTIONS

1. Boil 1 gallon of water and stir in the sugar to dissolve. Add the tea bags and let the tea steep for at least 30 minutes, then add the berries. Cool the tea in an ice bath to bring it to room temperature.

2. Once the tea is cool, remove the tea bags and stir in the starter kombucha. Pour the mixture into a 1-gallon glass jar and gently slide the SCOBY into the jar with clean hands. Cover the mouth of the jar with cheesecloth and secure it with a rubber band.

3. Keep the jar at room temperature, out of direct sunlight, and let it ferment for a week to 10 days. Check the jar periodically. A new SCOBY should start forming on the surface of the kombucha within a few days, usually attached to the old one. You might be unsettled by the sight of sediment and other random junk floating around in the jar, but this is all totally normal. Kombucha is a living thing.

4. After about a week, begin tasting the kombucha every day by pouring a little out of the jar. When it reaches a balance of sweetness and tartness that works for you, it's time to bottle. Before you bottle, get your next batch of kombucha ready, following the same steps as above. Remove the SCOBY and add it to the new batch.

5. Measure out your starter tea from this batch of kombucha to use next time. Pour the fermented kombucha into bottles. Leave about an inch of headspace in each bottle.

6. Store the bottled kombucha in a cool, dark place to carbonate. It should take about 3 or 4 days. Put the bottles in the refrigerator to stop fermentation. Your kombucha should last about a month or so.

Turmeric Green Tea Kombucha

Batch size: 1 gallon

Turmeric and green tea are both widely lauded for their healing properties on their own. Putting them together in a probiotic drink may just be the healthiest thing you've ever tasted.

INGREDIENTS

1 cup table sugar

8 bags green tea

½ ounce freshly grated turmeric or ½ teaspoon turmeric powder

2 cups kombucha from previous batch (or unpasteurized store-bought kombucha)

1 SCOBY per fermentation jar

INSTRUCTIONS

1. Boil 1 gallon of water and stir in the sugar to dissolve. Add the tea bags and let the tea steep for at least 30 minutes, then add the turmeric. Cool the tea in an ice bath to bring it to room temperature.

2. Once the tea is cool, remove the tea bags and stir in the starter kombucha. Pour the mixture into a 1-gallon glass jar and gently slide the SCOBY into the jar with clean hands. Cover the mouth of the jar with cheesecloth and secure it with a rubber band.

3. Keep the jar at room temperature, out of direct sunlight, and let it ferment for a week to 10 days. Check the jar periodically. A new SCOBY should start forming on the surface of the kombucha within a few days, usually attached to the old one. You might be unsettled by the sight of sediment and other random junk floating around in the jar, but this is all totally normal. Kombucha is a living thing.

continued

4. After about a week, begin tasting the kombucha every day by pouring a little out of the jar. When it reaches a balance of sweetness and tartness that works for you, it's time to bottle. Before you bottle, get your next batch of kombucha ready, following the same steps as above. Remove the SCOBY and add it to the new batch.

5. Measure out your starter tea from this batch of kombucha to use next time. Pour the fermented kombucha into bottles. Leave about an inch of headspace in each bottle.

6. Store the bottled kombucha in a cool, dark place to carbonate. It should take about 3 or 4 days. Put the bottles in the refrigerator to stop fermentation. Your kombucha should last about a month or so.

Raspberry Lemon Ginger Kombucha

Batch size: 1 gallon

Raspberry, lemon, and ginger are a trio of flavors that complement each other beautifully. The sweet yet tart raspberry, the bright lemon, and the spicy ginger blend with the sour bitterness of the kombucha to make one of my favorite tonics.

INGREDIENTS

1 cup table sugar

8 bags black tea

½ pint raspberries, chopped

1 tablespoon ginger

1 lemon, juiced and peeled

2 cups kombucha from previous batch (or unpasteurized store-bought kombucha)

1 SCOBY per fermentation jar

INSTRUCTIONS

1. Boil 1 gallon of water and stir in the sugar to dissolve. Add the tea bags and let the tea steep for at least 30 minutes, then add the raspberries, ginger, lemon juice, and lemon peel. Cool the tea in an ice bath to bring it to room temperature.

2. Once the tea is cool, remove the tea bags and stir in the starter kombucha. Pour the mixture into a 1-gallon glass jar and gently slide the SCOBY into the jar with clean hands. Cover the mouth of the jar with cheesecloth and secure it with a rubber band.

3. Keep the jar at room temperature, out of direct sunlight, and let it ferment for a week to 10 days. Check the jar periodically. A new SCOBY should start forming on the surface of the kombucha within a few days, usually attached to the old one. You might be unsettled by the sight of sediment and other random junk floating around in the jar, but this is all totally normal. Kombucha is a living thing.

4. After about a week, begin tasting the kombucha every day by pouring a little out of the jar. When it

continued

reaches a balance of sweetness and tartness that works for you, it's time to bottle. Before you bottle, get your next batch of kombucha ready, following the same steps as above. Remove the SCOBY and add it to the new batch.

5. Measure out your starter tea from this batch of kombucha to use next time. Pour the fermented kombucha into bottles. Leave about an inch of headspace in each bottle.

6. Store the bottled kombucha in a cool, dark place to carbonate. It should take about 3 or 4 days. Put the bottles in the refrigerator to stop fermentation. Your kombucha should last about a month or so.

Kefir

Kefir has recently burst back on to the health food scene. Sporting all the probiotic power and sour sweetness of its spoonable cousin, yogurt, kefir is a drinkable, portable, and equally delicious milk fermentation. But the milk kefir that probably springs to your mind is only one iteration. Water kefir is equally common, thriving in sugar-rich fruit-and-water solutions.

Kefir is made from tiny "grains"—in reality, small and rubbery SCOBYs made of bacteria and fungi. To the naked eye they look like translucent balls, but up close you can see the cauliflower-like folds that make up the symbiotic connections. As in kombucha, these various microbes combine to pool their efforts to break down their medium. The exact interplay between these microorganisms has yet to be fully fleshed out, but however it works, the grains reproduce like a single entity. And like kombucha, you can buy the grains from health food stores, homebrew shops, online retailers, or get your microbiome-obsessed friend to share some from her latest batch.

Kefir grains are needy little creatures. While yeast and bacteria will go dormant in the absence of food, the ties that bind the kefir colonies together don't handle famine well. Leave them without nourishment for even a week or two, and they'll quickly shrivel and die. But with a steady supply of milk or fruit, these little guys will keep pumping out tasty, healthy drinks for years to come.

Milk Kefir

Batch size: 1 quart

This drinkable yogurt makes a great breakfast on the go. Use this recipe as a base and add your favorite fruit for a more complete morning meal.

INGREDIENTS

4 cups milk

1 tablespoon milk kefir grains

INSTRUCTIONS

1. Pour the milk into a quart-sized Mason jar and stir in the kefir grains. Cover the jar with cheesecloth and secure with a rubber band.

2. Store the jar in a cool, dark place and let it ferment for at least 12 hours. Check to see if it has thickened to a consistency between buttermilk and yogurt. If too thin, let it sit up to another 24 hours.

3. When you've achieved the desired consistency, strain out the kefir grains and collect the kefir in a clean jar. Seal the container and store it in the refrigerator for up to 2 weeks.

Ryazhenka

Ryazehenka, or "baked milk," is a traditional fermented milk beverage from Eastern Europe. The name comes from the long simmering process, usually done in a low-temperature oven, that gives the milk a distinctive off-white hue and caramel flavor. After the baking process, kefir grains add a touch of sourness and a creamy texture.

INGREDIENTS

4 cups milk
1 tablespoon milk kefir grains

INSTRUCTIONS

1. Preheat the oven to 300°F. Pour the milk into a medium oven-safe baking dish and bake for 30 minutes.

2. When the milk turns golden brown, remove and cool to room temperature. Transfer to a quart-sized Mason jar and stir in the kefir grains. Cover the jar with cheesecloth and secure with a rubber band.

3. Store the jar in a cool, dark place and let it ferment for at least 12 hours. Check to see if it has thickened to a consistency between buttermilk and yogurt. If too thin, let it sit up to another 24 hours.

4. When you've achieved the desired consistency, strain out the kefir grains and collect the ryazhenka in a clean jar. Seal the container and store it in the refrigerator for up to 2 weeks.

Water Kefir

Batch size: 1 quart

Water kefir may not really be "kefir," but the process is pretty much the same even if the medium is different. Make sure you use water kefir grains and not milk kefir grains, as they are different animals.

INGREDIENTS

3 ounces brown sugar

2 tablespoons water kefir grains

INSTRUCTIONS

1. Add 4 cups of water to a saucepan and bring it to a boil. Remove from the heat and stir in the sugar to dissolve. Set aside to cool.

2. When the solution has cooled to room temperature, pour the sugar water into a quart-sized Mason jar and stir in the kefir grains. Cover the jar with cheesecloth and secure with a rubber band.

3. Store the jar in a cool, dark place and let it ferment for at least 12 hours. Check to see if it has thickened to a consistency between buttermilk and yogurt. If too thin, let it sit up to another 24 hours.

4. When you've achieved the desired consistency, strain out the kefir grains and collect the kefir in a clean jar. Seal the container and store it in the refrigerator for up to 2 weeks.

Coconut Mango Kefir

Batch size: 1 quart

Water kefir grains also work well in coconut water. Add some sliced mango and this becomes a tropical-infused treat.

INGREDIENTS

1 ripe mango

4 cups coconut water

1 tablespoon water kefir grains

INSTRUCTIONS

1. Dice the mango into a quart-sized Mason jar. Pour in the coconut water and stir in the kefir grains. Cover the jar with cheesecloth and secure with a rubber band.

2. Store the jar in a cool, dark place and let it ferment for at least 12 hours. With the sugar from the coconut water and the mango, it will ferment quickly and may suddenly begin to turn sour, so check periodically for taste.

3. When you've achieved the desired flavor, strain out the kefir grains and mango pieces and collect the kefir in a clean jar. It may continue to ferment even in the refrigerator, so make sure you leave headspace in the jar and do not tighten the lid all the way.

Kvass

Kvass is a popular drink from the Old World. The shtetls of Eastern Europe were once overflowing with this sour, bread-based tonic. And it's no wonder, once you understand how it's made. Like French toast (*pain perdu* en français, meaning "lost bread"), kvass is a way to use old, stale bread to make something else that tastes great. The bread is first toasted to dry it out completely, then submerged in water to extract the starchy, glutinous flavors within. A dash of acid and salt balances out the flavors before some additional sugar kick-starts a quick fermentation. The resulting sour, bubbly beverage tastes like a meal in a glass.

If you are an experienced baker who makes your own sourdough at home, then you have a leg up on your homebrewing colleagues with this one. You can use your sourdough starter as the fermentation agent and make a truly traditional brew. But for the rest of us, just a simple packet of champagne yeast will do the trick.

Sourdough Soda

Batch size: 1 gallon

This sour, bready tonic goes great with borscht and a hot bratwurst.

INGREDIENTS

1 loaf sourdough bread, stale

1 teaspoon salt

½ cup sugar

1 lemon, juiced

1 packet Champagne yeast

INSTRUCTIONS

1. Preheat the oven to 200°F. Chop the bread into large chunks and spread out on a cookie sheet or baking pan. Toast the bread for 15 minutes or until completely dried and crumbly. Meanwhile, boil 1 gallon of water on the stovetop and allow to cool to room temperature.

2. Once the bread and water are both cooled, place the bread in a large Mason jar and pour the water over the bread until it is submerged. Cover with cheesecloth, and let it sit overnight.

3. The next day, strain the bread and collect the liquid. To wring out all the liquid from the bread pieces, collect them in the cheesecloth and squeeze into your collected liquid. Add the salt, ¼ cup of sugar, lemon juice, and yeast, and stir gently to combine.

4. Pour into a 1-gallon jug with an airlock and place in a cool, dark place to ferment. Fermentation should be quick, taking less than a week for bubbling to subside.

5. Once fermentation is complete, add the remaining ¼ cup of sugar and stir to combine. Bottle and let sit for 2 days to carbonate, then place in the refrigerator.

Caraway Rye Kvass

Batch size: 1 gallon

Rye and caraway seeds add a bit of spice to this sour soda.

INGREDIENTS

1 loaf rye bread, stale
2 tablespoons caraway seeds, toasted
1 teaspoon salt
½ cup sugar
1 packet Champagne yeast

INSTRUCTIONS

1. Preheat the oven to 200°F. Chop the bread into large chunks and spread out on a cookie sheet or baking pan. Sprinkle caraway seeds over the top, distributing evenly. Toast the bread and seeds for 15 minutes or until completely dried and crumbly. Meanwhile, boil 1 gallon of water on the stovetop and allow to cool to room temperature.

2. Once the bread and water are both cooled, place the bread in a large Mason jar and pour the water over the bread until it is submerged. Cover with cheesecloth, and let it sit overnight.

3. The next day, strain the bread and collect the liquid. To wring out all the liquid from the bread pieces, collect them in the cheesecloth and squeeze into your collected liquid. Add the salt, ¼ cup of sugar, and yeast, and stir gently to combine.

4. Pour into a 1-gallon jug with an airlock and place in a cool, dark place to ferment. Fermentation should be quick, taking less than a week for bubbling to subside.

5. Once fermentation is complete, add the remaining ¼ cup of sugar and stir to combine. Bottle and let sit for 2 days to carbonate, then place in the refrigerator.

Beet "Kvass"

Batch size: 1 quart

The juice from vegetable fermentations carries many of the same flavors as kvass. This salty, sour, deep purple drink will satisfy all your pickle cravings.

INGREDIENTS

2 large beets

1 teaspoon salt

INSTRUCTIONS

1. Chop the beets into half-inch cubes and place them in a 1-quart Mason jar. Add the salt and 4 cups of water, making sure that all the cubes are completely submerged.

2. Cover with cheesecloth, and place the jar in a cool, dark place to ferment. Check on it once a day to make sure no mold has formed on the surface and that the beets remain submerged.

3. After a few days, the liquid will become a deep purple. Strain out the beets and enjoy this tart, probiotic tonic.

Carrot Ginger Parsnip "Kvass"

Batch size: 1 quart

Mixed vegetable fermentations are great for this kind of "kvass" because the flavors comingle in the brine. This is one of my favorite pickles anyway, so the fact that the brine is also tasty is a bonus.

INGREDIENTS

2 medium carrots

1 large parsnip

1 tablespoon ginger, minced

1 teaspoon salt

INSTRUCTIONS

1. Slice the carrots and parsnips into half-inch thick circles and place them in a 1-quart Mason jar with the minced ginger. Add the salt and water to cover, making sure that all the vegetables are completely submerged.

2. Place the jar in a cool, dark place to ferment. Check on it once a day to make sure no mold has formed on the surface and that the vegetables remain submerged.

3. After a few days, the liquid will become a deep purple. Strain out the carrots, parsnips, and ginger, and enjoy this tart, probiotic tonic.

Natural Soda

Fun fact: The original soda pop was a fermented beverage. The term "soft drink" comes from the idea that these fizzy, carbonated beverages were not "hard drinks" like their alcoholic brethren. Coke and Pepsi have subsequently removed all of the fermented goodness from their sodas, replacing them with sugar and unpronounceable chemicals. But you can ditch the fake CO_2 and get back to soda's natural origins at home.

Ginger Beer

Batch size: ½ gallon

Ginger beer is one of the original homemade soft drinks. If you want to embrace this drink's wild roots, try culturing the natural yeasts from ginger—called a ginger bug—instead of adding yeast.

INGREDIENTS

2 tablespoons fresh ginger, minced

½ cup table sugar

½ teaspoon kosher salt

½ cup fresh lime juice

½ packet Champagne yeast

INSTRUCTIONS

1. Place 3 cups of water along with the minced ginger, sugar, and salt in a saucepan and bring to a boil. Simmer the mixture for about 5 minutes, until the sugar is dissolved.

2. Remove from the heat and add 5 more cups of water. Place the pot in a quick ice bath to cool it to room temperature, then add the fresh lime juice and yeast.

3. Transfer to a clean (and sanitized!) 2-liter plastic bottle. Squeeze the bottle to remove as much air as possible, and screw on the cap. Ferment at room temperature until the bottle has fully expanded and is firm to the touch, which should only take a day or so. Leave it out on the counter for this step so you don't forget to check it.

4. Twist the cap to relieve a bit of the pressure, and then transfer to the refrigerator to stop fermentation. Enjoy!

Hibiscus Lemon Soda

Batch size: ½ gallon

Hibiscus flowers give this drink its distinctive color and flavor.

INGREDIENTS

2 tablespoons fresh ginger, minced

1 teaspoon dried hibiscus flowers

½ cup table sugar

½ teaspoon kosher salt

½ cup fresh lemon juice

½ packet Champagne yeast

INSTRUCTIONS

1. Place 3 cups of water along with the minced ginger, dried hibiscus flowers, sugar, and salt in a saucepan and bring to a boil. Simmer the mixture for about 5 minutes, until the sugar is dissolved.

2. Remove from the heat and add 5 more cups of water. Place the pot in a quick ice bath to cool it to room temperature, then add the fresh lemon juice and yeast.

3. Transfer to a clean (and sanitized!) 2-liter plastic bottle. Squeeze the bottle to remove as much air as possible, and screw on the cap. Ferment at room temperature until the bottle has fully expanded and is firm to the touch, which should only take a day or so. Leave it out on the counter for this step so you don't forget to check it.

4. Twist the cap to relieve a bit of the pressure, and then transfer to the refrigerator to stop fermentation. Enjoy!

Sarsaparilla

Batch size: ½ gallon

An antecedent of root beer, sarsaparilla is a beguiling concoction of sassafras, ginger, licorice, vanilla, cinnamon, and anise.

INGREDIENTS

1 ounce sassafras root, chopped

1 tablespoon fresh ginger, minced

1 ounce licorice root

1 vanilla bean or 1 teaspoon vanilla extract

1 cinnamon stick

1 teaspoon anise seed

½ cup table sugar

½ teaspoon kosher salt

½ packet Champagne yeast

INSTRUCTIONS

1. Place 3 cups of water along with the sassafras, ginger, licorice, vanilla, cinnamon, anise, sugar, and salt in a saucepan and bring to a boil. Simmer the mixture for about 5 minutes, until the sugar is dissolved.

2. Remove from the heat and add 5 more cups of water. Place the pot in a quick ice bath to cool it to room temperature, then add the yeast.

3. Transfer to a clean (and sanitized!) 2-liter plastic bottle. Squeeze the bottle to remove as much air as possible, and screw on the cap. Ferment at room temperature until the bottle has fully expanded and is firm to the touch, which should only take a day or so. Leave it out on the counter for this step so you don't forget to check it.

4. Twist the cap to relieve a bit of the pressure, and then transfer to the refrigerator to stop fermentation. Enjoy!

Grandpa's Celery Soda

Batch size: ½ gallon

For those who prefer more savory flavors in their soda, try this old-timey concoction.

INGREDIENTS

2 tablespoons celery seeds

½ cup table sugar

½ teaspoon kosher salt

½ cup fresh lime juice

½ packet Champagne yeast

INSTRUCTIONS

1. Place 3 cups of water along with the celery seeds, sugar, and salt in a saucepan and bring to a boil. Simmer the mixture for about 5 minutes, until the sugar is dissolved.

2. Remove from the heat and add 5 more cups of water. Place the pot in a quick ice bath to cool it to room temperature, then add the fresh lime juice and yeast.

3. Transfer to a clean (and sanitized!) 2-liter plastic bottle. Squeeze the bottle to remove as much air as possible, and screw on the cap. Ferment at room temperature until the bottle has fully expanded and is firm to the touch, which should only take a day or so. Leave it out on the counter for this step so you don't forget to check it.

4. Twist the cap to relieve a bit of the pressure, and then transfer to the refrigerator to stop fermentation. Enjoy!

Switchel

Switchel seems a fitting note on which to end this book, since it requires almost no work to create at home. A tonic based around vinegar, sugar, and spice, it has been a staple of home health remedies for centuries. If you are craving the tart flavors of fermentation but don't actually feel like waiting weeks for your beverage of choice, switchel can be whipped up in a matter of minutes. And its variations are almost limitless. Though typically made with a base of apple cider vinegar, any white vinegar such as white wine vinegar, rice wine vinegar, or even white balsamic vinegar would work just as well. The sugar can be anything from pure cane sugar to honey, maple syrup, or even fruit concentrate. Spices like ginger add bite, but you can adjust to your liking. You can even add spirits and make a shrub-like cocktail. Probiotics have never tasted so good.

Honey Lemon Switchel

Batch size: 1 gallon

A classic version of switchel, best mixed on a hot summer day.

INGREDIENTS

1 cup raw apple cider vinegar

½ cup raw honey

2 tablespoons ginger, grated

¼ cup lemon juice

1 lemon peel

INSTRUCTIONS

1. Combine the apple cider vinegar, honey, ginger, and lemon juice and peel in a gallon jug. Stir until the honey dissolves into solution.

2. Add 3 quarts of water and shake vigorously to combine. Let it sit at room temperature overnight for flavors to develop.

3. The next day, strain out the ginger and lemon peel, and collect the liquid in a separate jar. Serve over ice.

Maple Lime Switchel

Batch size: 1 gallon

Maple and lime might not seem like the most obvious pairing, but trust me: It works.

INGREDIENTS

1 cup raw apple cider vinegar

½ cup grade A maple syrup

2 tablespoons fresh ginger, grated

¼ cup lime juice

1 lemon peel

INGREDIENTS

1. Combine the apple cider vinegar, maple syrup, ginger, lime juice, and lemon peel in a gallon jug. Stir until the maple syrup dissolves into solution.

2. Add 3 quarts of water and shake vigorously to combine. Let it sit at room temperature overnight for flavors to develop.

3. The next day, strain out the ginger and lemon peel, and collect the liquid in a separate jar. Serve over ice.

Cinnamon Maple Switchel

Batch size: 1 gallon

Maple and cinnamon are a breakfast tradition. This morning treat satisfies both sweet and sour alike.

INGREDIENTS

1 cup raw apple cider vinegar

½ cup grade A maple syrup

1 cinnamon stick

INSTRUCTIONS

1. Combine the apple cider vinegar, maple syrup, and cinnamon in a gallon jug. Stir until the maple syrup dissolves into solution.

2. Add 3 quarts of water and shake vigorously to combine. Let it sit at room temperature overnight for flavors to develop.

3. The next day, strain out the cinnamon and collect the liquid in a separate jar. Serve over ice.

Haymaker's Punch

Batch size: 1 gallon

Everything is better with a little touch of whiskey. Switchel is no exception.

INGREDIENTS

1 cup raw apple cider vinegar

½ cup raw honey

2 tablespoons ginger, grated

2 ounces rye whiskey

¼ cup lemon juice

1 lemon peel

1 dash cayenne pepper

INSTRUCTIONS

1. Combine the apple cider vinegar, honey, ginger, whiskey, lemon juice, lemon peel, and cayenne pepper in a gallon jug. Stir until the honey dissolves into solution.

2. Add 3 quarts of water and shake vigorously to combine. Let it sit at room temperature overnight for flavors to develop.

3. The next day, strain out the ginger and collect the liquid in a separate jar. Serve over ice.

Books

Brew Like a Monk: Trappist, Abbey, and Strong Belgian Ales and How to Brew Them by Stan Hieronymous (Brewer's Publications, 2005)

Brooklyn Brew Shop's Beer Making Book: 52 Seasonal Recipes for Small Batches by Erica Shea and Stephen Valand (Clarkson Potter, 2011)

Cider, Hard & Sweet: History, Traditions, and Making Your Own by Ben Watson (Countryman, 2013)

Cider: Making, Using, and Enjoying Sweet & Hard Cider by Annie L. Proulx and Lew Nichols (Storey, 2003)

Craft Cider: How to Turn Apples into Alcohol by Jeff Smith (Countryman, 2015)

Farmhouse Ales: Culture and Craftsmanship in the Belgian Tradition by Phil Markowski (Brewer's Publications, 2004)

How to Brew: Everything You Need to Know to Brew Great Beer Every Time by John J. Palmer (Brewer's Publications, 4th Edition 2017)

Make Mead Like a Viking: Traditional Techniques for Brewing Natural, Wild-Fermented Honey-Based Wines and Beers by Jereme Zimmerman (Chelsea Green, 2015)

Nourishing Traditions: The Cookbook that Challenges Politically Correct Nutrition and Diet Dictocrats by Sally Fallon with Mary G. Enig, PhD (Newtrends Publishing, 2001)

The Art of Fermentation: An In-Depth Exploration of Essential Concepts and Processes from Around the World by Sandor Ellix Katz (Chelsea Green, 2014)

The Compleat Meadmaker: Home Production of Honey Wine from Your First Batch to Award-Winning Fruit by Ken Schramm (Brewer's Publications, 2003)

The Complete Joy of Home Brewing by Charlie Papazian (Harper, 2014)

The Homebrewer's Almanac: A Seasonal Guide to Making Your Own Beer from Scratch by Marika Josephson, Aaron Kleidon, and Ryan Tockstein (Countryman, 2016)

The Homebrewer's Garden: How to Grow, Prepare, and Use Your Own Hops, Malts, and Brewing Herbs by Joe Fisher and Dennis Fisher (Storey, 2016)

True Brews: How to Craft Fermented Cider, Beer, Wine, Sake, Soda, Mead, Kefir, and Kombucha at Home by Emma Christensen (Ten Speed Press, 2013)

Suppliers

BEER, CIDER & MEAD

Brooklyn Brew Shop
www.brooklynbrewshop.com
Midwest Supplies
www.midwestsupplies.com
Northern Brewer
www.northernbrewer.com

SAKE

Home Brew Sake
www.homebrewsake.com
Vision Brewing
www.visionbrewing.com

NONALCOHOLIC

Cultures for Health
www.culturesforhealth.com
Kombucha Brooklyn
www.kombuchabrooklyn.com

Blogs

Bear Flavored
www.bear-flavored.com
The Mad Fermentationist
www.themadfermentationist.com

ACKNOWLEDGMENTS

Thank you to all the professionals who took time to speak with me: Derek Dellinger at Kent Falls Brewing Company in Kent, Connecticut; Max Pritchard at Breezy Hill Orchard in Staatsburg, New York; Jason Kallicragas at the BottleHouse Brewing Company in Cleveland Heights, Ohio; and Jeff Bell at Texas Sake in Austin, Texas.

Thank you to the fantastic team at Countryman: editorial director Ann Treistman, my editor Michael Tizzano, production manager Devon Zahn, production editor Jess Murphy, cover designer Anna Reich, and publicist Devorah Backman.

Thank you to all my friends and family who graciously (and bravely) sampled my test batches throughout this process. Couldn't have done this without all of you.

And the biggest thank you to my wife, Colleen, who allowed our apartment to become a fermentation laboratory for more than a year. I look forward to spending the rest of my life brewing you session IPAs and dry farmhouse ales.

INDEX